ART AND PRUDENCE

Publications of the Jacques Maritain Center

1

ART AND PRUDENCE

STUDIES IN THE THOUGHT OF JACQUES MARITAIN

Ralph McInerny

UNIVERSITY OF NOTRE DAME PRESS

NOTRE DAME, INDIANA

Library of Congress Cataloging-in-Publication Data

McInerny, Ralph M.
    Art and prudence: studies in the thought of Jacques Maritain/
Ralph McInerny.
        p.   cm.— (Publications of the Jacques Maritain Center; 1)
    ISBN 0-268-00619-9, ISBN 0-268-00620-2 (pbk.)
    1. Maritain, Jacques, 1882–1973. I. Title. II. Series.
BX4705.M3993M45 1988
194—dc19   88-18826

Manufactured in the United States of America

IN MEMORIAM
Professor Joseph Evans
Director of Notre Dame's Maritain Center
1957-1979

CONTENTS

PREFACE

UN PETIT TOUR DE MARITAIN

Jacques Maritain was born in Paris on November 18, 1882 and died in Toulouse on April 28, 1973. His long life combined the hermetic withdrawal of the scholar and the limelight of the diplomat, the skills of a controversialist and the art of lecturing; both metaphysician and political philosopher, he had a marriage of mythic proportions and, at the end, a vocation as a Little Brother of Jesus; he counted Paul VI among his friends as well as Saul Alinsky, and from first to last, whatever engaged him, his was a life combining prayer and intelligence. Furthermore, from 1910 when he published his first article ("La science moderne et la raison.") until his death -- *Les approches sans entraves* was published posthumously -- writing came as naturally to him as breathing.

There are innumerable ports of entry to the thought of Maritain. Some have been attracted by his aesthetics, others by his political philosophy; his metaphysics captivates others and for many his conception of Christian Philosophy and how to be a Thomist in the contemporary world has provided a map for their own lives; his *Notebook* and *Raissa's Journal* as well as her memoirs, *We Have Been Friends Together* and *Adventures in Grace*, open up the special world of the French Catholic intellectual, at the bottom of which is always a burning desire for sanctity.

In this book I bring together a number of studies of the thought of Maritain which were written for different occasions with no thought of eventually bringing them together between covers. Yet when I looked over what I had written about Maritain, with an eye to a collection, I was surprised that I had written so much and struck by the fact that it was largely by way of his work in aesthetics and moral philosophy that I approached Maritain. Of course it is true that any approach will eventually link up with all the major themes of Maritain's thought. Nonetheless, his writings on art and morals are both interesting in themselves and a way into Maritain's lifelong effort to express the perennial philosophy.

It can even be said that this is the front door of the edifice Maritain was to build, since if we except his study of the thought of Bergson, *Art and Scholasticism*, published in 1920, is his first book. It is certainly the first book in which in a nonpolemical way he emerges as a Thomist. The previous year, the Maritains had begun in their home those reunions from which would emerge the *Cercles thomistes*. Indeed, when one looks at this little book, which like so many others of Maritain would go through a series of editions, taking on appendices and notes along the way, one is struck by its, well, scholasticism. I mean that its manner as well as its substance is scholastic, with passage after passage transported entire from medieval Latin into Maritain's French. He proceeds in the serene confidence that discussions in the *Summa theologiae* have contemporary relevance and can cast light on questions undreamt of in the 13th Century. The impact the book continues to have, not only on theoreticians but on working artists, justifies his confidence.

Thus, having recalled the distinction between the theoretical and practical, he locates art as a virtue of practical intellect, and discusses the contrast of servile and liberal arts. Like Aristotle and Thomas Aquinas before him, Maritain sees art as a skill in making, in altering a naturally given material either to facilitate natural ends or for purposes undreamt of by nature. The artist is first of all someone who makes things. Only when this has been established, does he introduce the concept of beauty and of the fine arts. In short, "art" is not a univocal but an analogous term, possessing an ordered set of meanings ranging from the making of shoes to the writing of tragedy. Features of art in its humblest but most accessible sense are modified and extended to the higher forms of art. In this context, logic too is an art, and we find Maritain comparing logic and fine art, pondering the question of imitation and then turning to two themes that will preoccupy him throughout his career, the relation between art and faith and the relation between art and religion.

Art and Scholasticism provided the sure foundation for all Maritain's later work in aesthetics. In subsequent writings, he would take into account what we might call the difference between the technique of an art and its content. That is, he came to see that there are limitations on thinking of a fine art in terms of the skill required to make the artifact. After all, something of the technique of any art -- the terminological redundancy is itself significant -- can be learned by many but surely not everyone who profits from instruction in painting or writing or composing is thereby an artist. *Poetae nascuntur*. In any art, it is possible for lesser talents to introduce technical variations, to carry to a more complete perfection the technique of the genre, and be for all that minor figures. The difference lies in the fact that the major figure has a distinctive voice thanks to which we hear what we had not heard before and yet, having heard it, experience the shock of recognition.

Had Maritain simply extended the notion of art as skill in making to the fine arts, he would have run the risk of putting a premium on mere technique. But his attention turned increasingly to what the poet had to say and the sources of his knowledge. In a 1935 collection of essays, the titular essay , "The Frontiers of Poetry" (*Art and Scholasticism and The Frontiers of Poetry*, translated by Joseph Evans, Notre Dame University Press, 1974) considers the way in which poetry is limited by non-poetry, *i.e.* all that which is beyond the rules and techniques of art. "On Poetic Knowledge: De la connaissance poetique," appeared in a 1938 book containing pieces by both Raissa and Jacques. It is in this essay that we find Maritain talking of poetic knowledge in terms of connaturality, a topic discussed in several essays included below.

From this point on, Maritain's interest in art centers on the creative intuition out of which the artifact emerges. His views reach their definitive statement in the Mellon Lectures delivered in the National Gallery of Art in Washington in the Spring of 1952, published as *Creative Intuition in Art and Poetry*. It is fitting that a philosophical reflection on art which took its rise from the thought of St. Thomas Aquinas should culminate in a discussion of Dante.

If there is any poet whose vision was shaped by

religious faith and a comprehensive philosophy as well, that poet is Dante. For Maritain he is the supreme poet, in part because the *Divine Comedy* contains in unity what was to divide and become three kinds of poetry: Song, Drama, the Novel. The discussion of Dante in the Mellon Lectures is the culmination of a lifetime's reflection on art. In it we find developed what in earlier writings had been merely inchoate and there is much to be said for tracking the evolution of Maritain's aesthetics through its many stages. This is no philosopher willing to grant poetry some role ancillary to his system. For man, art is not a frill, an option, but essential to what he is. In the sense of *homo faber*, of course, but understanding making as extending analogously from the reworking of hide into a writing material to the canto then inscribed upon the vellum. In reflecting on Dante, Maritain's attention turns to the creative source from which the 100 cantos of the *Comedy* come. That connatural intuition of the poet has as its medium his subjectivity, but it is an intuition of what is. Maritain will unabashedly call it ontological.

Given Maritain's Catholicism and Thomism, we may think it inevitable that Dante should be for him the poet *par excellence*. But we would be wrong were to imagine that Maritain sees the *Divine Comedy* as, in that unfortunate phrase, the *Summa theologiae* in verse. Dante's faith and the medieval hierarchical vision of reality are part of what Dante is, part of his sensibility; they do not function in the poem as a preexistent material to which he is merely giving linguistic shape. Unbelievers respond to the poetry of Dante and contemporary poets in number try their hand at translating the *Comedy*. A corollary of the truth that poets are born is that they are born at quite specific times and places. Dante was lucky in both regards,

Maritain asserts, and there is little doubt that he has in mind a truth that transcends poetry when he says that. But he will not confuse the truth of poetry with the truth of Christianity.

No doubt this explains Maritain's almost eager openness to modern art and poetry. He is not the first to compare Dante and Baudelaire, but no one has managed a more subtle balance of the poet and his times, the poet and personal morality, the poet and an ambience of faith or its opposite. There is an innocence deep down any poet, Maritain maintains, and every poet is in possession of existential certitudes, extremely simple, extremely profound, which are of the essence of poetic intuition. What are they? That existence is irreducibly mysterious yet possesses intelligibility. The interiority and importance of human existence. The certitude that between man and the world there is a link deeper than any material one. That man's freedom lends direction and orientation to his life, which can never be lost in a void, and which implicates the whole of being. Every poet exhibits these existential certitudes.

Needless to say, like any theory of art, Maritain's view is at once empirical and a standard of admission. But he is a constant source of surprise in his selection of artists. (*Creative Intuition in Art and Poetry* is studded with what he calls Texts without Commentaries, poems, passages from St. Thomas, reproductions of paintings.)

When we see Maritain's aesthetic develop from its initial emphasis on making to concentration on the subjective source of art, we do well to ask how he can claim to know what he tells us about poetic intuition, the subjectivity of the poet which possesses affective connaturality with reality. Since he makes no claim to be an artist, he could not make appeal to introspection. Or does his tribute to Raissa, who was a poet, mean that he relied on introspection at secondhand? Not at all. Jacques Maritain was from first to last a disciple of Aristotle and Thomas and a foe of all idealism in epistemology. The primary source for his reflections on art is -- the artifact. We have no other means, he insists, to speculate on the subjectivity of the poet.

In short, there is a fundamental unity in Maritain's aesthetics, a sense in which making and the artifact are always the focus of attention. The essays of mine I include here do not pretend to provide a complete let alone exhaustive account of Maritain's aesthetics. But I will be content if they attract even more readers to this far from neglected aspect of his achievement.

By the same token, what the following essays have to say about Maritain's moral philosophy does not convey anything like the full picture of his contributions, which are historical as well as theoretical. I am especially conscious of the absence of any discussion of Maritain's notion of Moral Philosophy Adequately Considered. But that is an aspect of his conception of Christian Philosophy and I find myself returning to that theme, one I had thought sufficiently worked, because of my reading in Edith Stein. My intention is that these reflections, prompted chiefly by *Endliches und ewiges Sein*, will eventually find their way into print.

I dedicate this book to my late colleague Joe Evans, the first director of the Jacques Maritain Center at Notre Dame, and a man whose influence lives on, not only in his translations of Maritain, but also in generations of students whose tributes to his teaching and talk continue to edify me.

Support for the publication of this book was received from the National Endowment for the Humanities.

ONE

THE INTELLECTUAL VOCATION
OF JACQUES MARITAIN

It may seem paradoxical that philosophy, taken as the theoretical use of our reason aimed at conceptual clarification and cogent argument, both utterly impersonal, should nonetheless, in its concrete role in human culture, bear the indelible stamp of the philosopher himself. It would be a peculiar argument that depended for its validity on the fact that so-and-so formulated it, as if *ipse dixit* were one of its premisses. However, if authority is the weakest argument in philosophy, it is nevertheless undeniable that some philosophers speak with an authority that transcends the content of what they say taken simply as such. For well over half a century, Jacques Maritain's voice was one to which others attended, giving ear to what was said at least at the outset *because* of the person saying it. Reflecting on why this was true in his case turns out to be a good way of drawing attention to the nature of his achievement and the character of his contribution.

What strikes one about Jacques Maritain, what to a great degree explains the enormous influence he had, and has, is the fusion in him of the intellectual and spiritual lives. He did not view the cultivation of his mind as a pursuit which was separate, however much it might be distinct, from the more existential task of becoming what he was called to be. In order to see this, we must look into his autobiography but, at the same time, we should notice that he provided us with an account, on a more theoretical level, of this fusion and of the need for it.

I believe that it is out of this union of his intellectual life with the pursuit of sanctity that Maritain's lively sense of the variety, yet interrelatedness, of uses of the mind arose. He insisted on the analogical diversity of cultural activities and that of course meant that there was both plurality and unity. *Les degres de savoir* is the basic reference for this concept, but it must be supplemented by several later works. *Sapientis est ordinare.* Maritain's far-ranging interests were not the diversionary pursuits of the dilettante. In appreciating the distinctiveness of science and metaphysics, ethics and poetry, dogmatic and mystical theology, Maritain saw as well the way in which they all hang together as so many modalities of man's vocation.

How radically the vitality of the Church prior to Vatican II seems to swing around the great converts to the faith! One thinks of Dorothy Day, Chesterton, Thomas Merton, and it is as if they form part of a line that goes back to Newman and includes Gerard Manley Hopkins as well. In the France of this century, Jacques Maritain is surely one of the chief converts to the faith. Who has not felt privy to the inner lives of Jacques and Raissa in reading *Les grandes amities* and *Les aventures de la grace?* Now these can be supplemented by the *Journal de Raissa* and Jacques' own *Carnet de notes*. Why is the recently published correspondence with Julien Green just the sort of epistolary exchange we expect from the man we meet in Raissa's memoirs? The answer to that and the simplest description of Jacques Maritain is: a man striving for sanctity.

The young couple who turned away from suicide after seriously considering it were not moved by *joie de vivre* or only by a return of animal good spirits. They were not reconciled to life until they could accept it as a gift from a loving creator. How improbable a means of their conversion Leon Bloy seems and yet, in God's providence, he was precisely the one to lead these young people to the faith, to become their godfather, to burn into their hearts the simple truth of *La femme pauvre*: there is but one tragedy, not to be a saint. No one could imagine Bloy tossing that off as a literary remark. It summed up his own deepest conviction. No one can understand Jacques Maritain who does not see that his overriding concern was to achieve union with God.

In recent years the connection between a person's being a philosopher and being a Catholic is thought of as accidental at best: these just happen to be true of the same person. Not only would it be thought strange to suggest that the connection might be more than contingent, even Catholic philosophers seem to have accepted the view that philosophy is indifferent, even hostile, to religious belief. At philosophical conventions, one senses the not altogether unstated conviction that serious use of the mind puts religious belief into jeopardy. A Catholic who lives professionally in this atmosphere can lead a schizophrenic existence. Worse, he may adopt an implicit fideism, the very antithesis of the Catholic view on the relation between faith and reason.

One of the great attractions of Maritain to people of
my generation was his serene confidence that the faith
enhances and strengthens the pursuit of even natural
truths: *philosophandum in fide*, in the phrase of John of
St. Thomas that Maritain adopted as a kind of motto.
The Catholic should not do philosophy sheepishly, as if,
unlike everyone else's, his mind is not a blank slate and
he is unwilling to follow the argument wherever it goes.
A programmatic skepticism has come to be regarded as
an integral part of the philosophic enterprise, as if one
could scarcely engage in it if he has antecedent
convictions, particularly if these convictions are a result
of the grace of faith.   How terrible for the believer to
accept the suggestion that his faith is an irrational
prejudice. Jacques Maritain was there to remind us that
faith is an all but practical *necessity* if we are to achieve
with sureness vital truths accessible in principle to
natural reason.

Who could look at the history of philosophy and
conclude that all is right with the human mind,
particularly when of late that history so largely consists
of claims that all of a philosopher's predecessors have
been in error? The thought of the Middle Ages, so airily
dismissed by a Bertrand Russell, for example, when
examined in its own setting and without the prejudices
of the supposedly unprejudiced philosopher, can seem a
high point in the history of western thought rather than
an aberrant episode. In spite of this fact, we should not
think Jacques Maritain was turning toward the past
when he turned to St. Thomas Aquinas.

Actually it seems to have been Raissa who first began
to read Thomas and she read him as she read Albertus
Magnus, in continuity with her effort to make progress
in prayer. *La vie d'oraison*, the little work co-authored by
Jacques and Raissa, is called in English, *Prayer and
Intelligence*.   This work embodies the point I wish to
make. The Maritains were addressing themselves to the

lay intellectual. They were actually saying that there is an essential connection between prayerful union with God and the effort to arrive at the good of the mind, namely, truth. Nothing could seem more remote from the conception of the philosophical life now regnant. Yet this insistence is actually a return to the great tradition in philosophy reaching back through the medieval and patristic periods into classical Greek philosophy. Think of the *Phaedo*, think of the *Protrepticus*, think of the *Consolation of Philosophy* and the *De modo studendi*. The virtuous life is a necessary but not sufficient condition for the successful theoretical use of the mind. Indeed, there are moral virtues peculiar to the intellectual life. Philosophizing is a vocation, not a career.

We know that Maritain decided against an academic career as a philosopher -- although, fortunately for us all he was not wholly to escape the "poison ivy" of our walls. We know that he and his wife took a vow to live together as brother and sister, foregoing the hope of progeny the better to devote themselves to the pursuit of sanctity. The *Journal de Raissa* gives us an insight into the prayer life to which both Maritains devoted themselves, from their conversion (1906) to the First World War. In 1914, as Jacques notes in Chapter V of the *Carnet de notes*, began those meetings at Meudon which would eventually take shape as the *Cercle d'etudes thomistes*. The amount of space devoted to the Cercle in the *Carnet de notes* (pp. 183-254, plus the appendix pp.393-405) indicates how large it loomed in Maritain's mind, both at the time the *Cercle* flourished and later when he was preparing his notebooks for publication.

In an entry for April 29, 1921, he wrote of the purpose of the Cercle:

> To help laypeople maintain the purity of Thomism and disseminate it. Members must resolve to be guided by St. Thomas with complete fidelity, to read the

Summa at least half an hour a day and to devote at least
half an hour a day to prayer. (p. 191)

Study and prayer. The two were to go hand in hand,
nor was   prayer to be thought of as merely a pious
addendum: it was essential to Maritain's conception of
the intellectual life. To underscore this, there was an
annual retreat for members of the *cercles thomistes*. These
retreats continued until the outbreak of war and
Maritain tells us that it was the war which effectively
put an end to the *Cercle d'etudes*. He goes on:

> I would like to dwell a bit on one of the more typical
> characteristics of the Thomistic Circles, namely the
> tight connection of the intellectual life and the spiritual
> life, the guarantee of which was the vow of prayer. By
> that means, as is stated in our statutes, this company of
> secular priests and laypeople had as the base of their
> activity a profound and intimate gift of the self to God.
> It offered to souls who aspired to perfection while
> remaining in the world a very real help without in any
> way infringing on anyone's freedom, since the vow of
> prayer concerned only the absolutely personal relation of
> God and the soul. (p. 235)

It is surprising to think of Jacques Maritain as a great
organizer and indeed in his retrospective remarks on
the *cercle thomistes* he insists on the *point* of the
organizing rather than the organization itself. The point
is to put the lay intellectual squarely in line with the
evangelizing task which falls chiefly on the shoulders of
bishops and clergy.

One is struck by the fact that when the Maritains
became Catholics they intended that everything they
should subsequently do must come into line with that
principal fact about their lives. There should be no
question of a few pious practices juxtaposed with

professional activity, a professorial career like any other but with Mass on Sundays. No, the Maritains became daily communicants, they conjoined their prayerful union with the Truth and the more abstract and concrete intellectual pursuits of truth. To pray well and to understand well are distinct, but ee separate only at our peril.

Perhaps this is enough to suggest why we cannot think of Jacques Maritain's pursuit of sanctity as unrelated to his philosophical and theological work. Whether we read of Jacques and Raissa in the first years of their Catholic lives devoting themselves to prayer as well as study, or go on to the origin and evolution of the *Cercles d'etudes*, or pursue them through the long story of their lives, there is a unified vision, of the way all things work together to the chief end.

Not only is the pursuit of sanctity paramount in Maritain's own life, I think it is as well the single simplest explanation of the appeal he had for so many Catholics engaged in the various aspects of culture and the intellectual life -- artists, theologians, poets, philosophers, novelists and contemplatives. Maritain put before us a version of the Catholic task which excited and stirred and strengthened the sense one had that the use of the mind is, after all, not the whole of life, be it ever so important. It was Claudel who said that "Youth is not made for pleasure but for heroism." This was a message Maritain too conveyed. In an era when doing philosophy had come to seem only a matter of winning arguments, it was nothing short of edifying to be reminded that it is rather an invitation to become wise. *O Sapientia*, was the motto of the *Cercles d'etudes*, and it had been adopted at Raissa's suggestion. But there are, of course, degrees of wisdom.

If it is the hundredth anniversary of Jacques Maritain, it is the fiftieth anniversary of the publication of *Les degres du savoir*. This is, without a doubt, Maritain's masterpiece. He wrote a dozen other books which, taken as wholes, are better books, but their aim is less lofty and their scope is much narrower. *Les degres du savoir* has both the strengths and the flaws of a masterpiece, but the flaws bother us no more than do lapses by Tolstoy and Shakespeare. At the age of fifty, Maritain produced a work of genius, what may prove to be a masterwork of neo-scholasticism or, to be more precise, of twentieth century Thomism.

The intensity of Maritain's devotion to St. Thomas, noticeable in the statues of the *Cercle d'etudes*, is best captured by his variation on the Pauline phrase : *Vae mihi si non thomistizavero*. The little *Introduction to philosophy* Maritain wrote does not prepare the reader for the creative and extended Thomism that characterizes Maritain's other work. *The Introduction* was the first philosophical work I read and I welcomed its schematic character, its definitions -- in short, its scholastic tone. The book might give the impression that Maritain thought that things were pretty much the same in the twentieth century as in the thirteenth century or even in the fourth century B.C.. This expectation might be intensified when one considered the profound dissatisfaction Maritain showed with modern thought. It would be a great mistake to think of *The Peasant of the Garrone* as the cranky work of an old man which is somehow out of continuity with his other writings. *Antimoderne* -- the very title is eloquent in that regard. Descartes, Luther, Rousseau, Hegel, Bergson, Heidegger, Husserl, the Positivists -- Maritain sets his face definitively against the main currents of modern thought. But this lack of sympathy with much of modern philosophy does not prevent Maritain from being extremely interested in the various aspects of contemporary culture nor from extending and developing his Thomism so that it becomes a more comprehensive and nuanced system than it was when he received it.

But before speaking of the extensions and prolongations and new applications Maritain made of the thought of Aquinas, we must draw attention to the fact that all this was preceded by a careful reading of the text. In the Jacques Maritain Center at Notre Dame, we have Maritain's copy of the two volume Marietti edition of Thomas's *Quaestio disputata de veritate*. There are marginalia on nearly every page and there are as well dozens of slips of paper on which Maritain outlined and analyzed the arguments of the text. We may be sure that when he spoke of reading the *Summa* for at least a half hour every day, he had in mind a similarly exegetical and close poring over the text. When Maritain extends the thought of Thomas into areas undreamed of by his mentor, we can be certain he is doing so on the basis of prolonged meditation on the texts of the Master.

Turning now to *Les degres du savoir*, let us recall its further title: *Distinguer pour unir ou Les degres du savoir*. The preface alerts us to Maritain's intention:

> Readers of these pages will perhaps perceive that even while maintaining in a rigorous fashion the formal note of St. Thomas's metaphysics and rejecting any sort of accommodation or dimunition meant to make Thomism *acceptable* to irrational prejudices, we have on several points tried to clear the terrain and move back the borders of the Thomistic synthesis. (p. xiv)

Characterizing Thomism a "an essentially progressive and assimilative doctrine," something which explains its influence on so many different minds and cultures, Maritain prepares us for the remarkable synthesis to follow.

What I have tried to suggest in the first part of this paper, the effective fusion of the intellectual and spiritual lives in Maritain, is something the reader senses in the opening discussion on the *grandeur et misere de la metaphysique*. From the very outset it is clear that for Maritain, the aim of philosophy is wisdom and the point of wisdom is to know God. "Sa grandeur: elle est sagesse. Sa misere: Elle est science humaine." (p. 3) There is as well, at the outset of this magisterial study, not much more than as an aside, still a striking comparison of the poet and the metaphysician): the intuition of the former compared with the intellectual perception of the latter. And there is the observation that a metaphysics which models itself on the current state of the sciences is bound to wither and die: as examples he mentions Descartes, Spinoza and Kant. But if Metaphysics is wisdom; it is not ultimate.

> Here then is the misery of metaphysics (and still more its grandeur). It stirs the desire for supreme union, a spiritual possession consummated in the order of reality itself, and not merely in idea. But it cannot satisfy it. *There is another wisdom that we preach, a scandal to the Jews and a folly to the Greeks.* Exceeding human effort, gift of a deifying grace and of the free largess of uncreated Wisdom, there is at its source that Wisdom's foolish love for each of us and at its term a unity of spirity with it. Only Jesus crucified, the Mediator lifted up between heaven and earth, gives access to it. (p. 15)

After this opening discussion no reader can fail to see that the volume in his hands is not a typical product of a contemporary lay philosopher. It is not simply that, in presenting and expanding the thought of St. Thomas, Maritain is taking into account that Thomas was a philosopher because he was a theologian and it is the latter function which is his principal one. That would imply that Maritain's achievement is simply to give an accurate historical narrative of what Thomas did. Far more than that is at issue here. Maritain at the outset of his study announces as intrinsically relevant for what *he* is doing the same religious faith as St. Thomas's. He is not reporting what was true of Thomas's convictions about a wisdom beyond human wisdom: Maritain is testifying to his own acceptance of the wisdom that comes to us only through the mediation of Jesus Christ.

Just as the fusion of the intellectual and spiritual in his life attracted many to Maritain, so too at a level of theoretical communication his programmatic assumption that the truths one accepts on faith must be put into relation with naturally achieved truths appeals to a Catholic who has felt the depressing redefinition of the intellectual life in a mode Maritain would likely describe as Platonist. This is the latter-day notion that the cultivation of the mind can be successfully pursued only in abstraction from the larger moral and existential tasks of the human person.

It came as no surprise to me that Maritain, in *Existence and the Existent*, felt affinity with some aspects of the thought of Kierkegaard. Indeed, it seemed to me that Maritain almost alone among Thomists saw that the Kierkegaardian emphasis on existence was to make a moral rather than a metaphysical point.

The first part of *Les degres du savoir* is concerned with degrees of rational knowing, that is, the achievements of unaided natural reason. Maritain discusses philosophy and experimental science, critical realism, philosophy of nature and metaphysics. Whatever else may be said of Maritain's effort to put together philosophy of nature in the traditional sense and experimental science, it is certainly one of the three major views formulated by Thomists in this century. Indeed, the other views were fashioned largely in reaction to Maritain's. Needless to say, Maritain's views on the nature of experimental science affect his views on the philosophy of nature, and vice versa. After his treatment of metaphysics, Maritain goes on to speak of *Les degres du savoir supra-rationnel.*

Under the rubric "mystical experience and philosophy," Maritain speaks of the wisdom of natural theology, the wisdom which is the revealed mysteries, theology as such, and finally the wisdom which is the gift of the Holy Ghost.

Les degres du savoir is a remarkable book, not simply for the range of its topics, but for the unity which animates the discussion. Consider what it is Maritain is suggesting. From man's engagement in the experimental sciences, seen as distinct from, yet related to, the familiar progression through the levels of philosophy to metaphysics, there is a single *elan*, a love and pursuit of wisdom, the desire to know and be united with God. In metaphysics, considered as natural theology, we have as it were a first and inadequate wisdom. Philosophy stirs our desire for union with God as he is in himself, but philosophy cannot satisfy that desire. Only thanks to the salvific action of Christ and the revelation of the mysteries of faith is there possible the wisdom, the theology, which reflects on those mysteries. But this is not the end. Beyond natural theology and scholastic theology is mystical union.

We are all familiar with the range of Maritain's masterpiece. Perhaps we are *too* familiar with it, and do not appreciate as once we did the power of its unifying vision. All the various topics hang together; they form a hierarchical order which honors their distinction one from another but not their separation. In discussing theology in the sense of reasoned reflection on the mysteries, Maritain remarks almost casually that the theologian who does not have a deep spiritual life, who has not had some mystical experience, could not meaningfully discuss mysticism. This is not to say that the theologian is thereby engaged in the analysis of his own experience as his own. Far from it. Nor for that matter is Maritain confusing the efforts of a St. Thomas Aquinas with those of a St. John of the Cross. But he is insisting that the things he distinguishes in his book finally cohere and form an order which is a new version of the Thomistic synthesis.

Maritain could not have written his masterwork if he did not have a lively sense of the different modes of knowing. There are adumbrations in this work of other daring prolongations of the doctrines he had found in Thomas Aquinas.

a) His reflections on the distinction between the speculative and the practical, and in particular on the degrees of practical knowledge, lead on to his distinctive conception of moral philosophy adequately considered.

b) Of greater importance is the justly famous way in which Maritain takes the conception of knowledge through *connaturality*, first encountered in St. Thomas, and elaborated by John of St. Thomas, applied in its original setting to moral knowledge and the knowledge of faith, and extends it to speak of poetic knowledge as a knowledge through connaturality.

I will argue in a later essay that Maritain's extension of the concept of knowledge by affective connaturality to poetic knowledge may present us with one of the best instances of the way in which he finds new applications of the thought of Thomas and engages in genuinely creative Thomism. The aesthetics of Maritain is a story in itself, in any case. Let us recognize that before Heidegger, Maritain was drawn to a fruitful comparison of the thinking of the poet and the thinking of the philosopher.

A more recent instance of the kind of attention to the variety of modes of knowing that seems to me to characterize Maritain's work is found in *Approches sans entraves*, Chap. XIII, "Le tenant-Lieu de theologie chez les simples." Indeed, each of the chapters brought together under *Pour epistemologie existentielle* shows us a Maritain continuing to cast the widest possible net as a Catholic thinker, to include and compare and make complementary activities which others simply failed to think together in the same thought.

You may perhaps be surprised that I have not given a place of privilege to what Maritain has to say of the intuition of being. This is not because I share the views of those who charge Maritain with being insufficiently alive to the centrality of the distinction of essence and existence in Thomism. Allied with this criticism is a criticism of the attention and honor Maritain paid Aristotle and those great Thomistic commentators Cardinal Cajetan and John of St. Thomas. I sometimes think that Maritain's critics lack his own sure sense of the way in which philosophy must be grounded in the common certainties of mankind. I am not always clear what is being proposed when I am told that the real distinction between essence and existence lies at the very heart of the thought of St. Thomas Aquinas and that an understanding of it is presupposed for the understanding of *everything* else he has to say. Surely that cannot be true if, as seems clear from any attempt to explicate it, the real distinction is an exceedingly recherche affair. When Maritain speaks of the intuition of being, he is clearly not referring to some metaphysical achievement of an esoteric sort. Here again his approach seems to me to be reminiscent of Heidegger and manifestly more attractive if only because more intelligible.

Why is there anything at all rather than nothing? This Leibnitzean query is put to good use by Heidegger. Taken just by itself it may be seen to function as a recalling of the wonder and surprise which are the appropriate responses to the very existence of things, ourselves included. In ordinary workaday life, perhaps necessarily, we take things for granted. One crossing a street would be ill advised to fall into rapturous wonder over the existence of a tree whose branches arch over the intersection. But there are appropriate times, and when we are about to do metaphysics is one of them. Then we do well to recapture our sense of wonder at existent things. I have often thought that the premisses of the Tertia Via make similar demands and that it is . possible to classify philosophers in terms of their response to the claim that not everything that exists can be like the things that are brought about as the effects of other caused things. A philosopher who has lost his sense of wonder will be puzzled as to why we cannot simply keep introducing things of that sort (effects) to explain other things of that sort . But the crucial move is to wonder why there should be *any* things of that sort.

The later writings of Jacques Maritain are, with few exceptions, theological in the narrow sense of the term: reasoned reflection on the mysteries of the faith. If thomas was a theologian who became a philosopher in order to be a better theologian, Jacques Maritain was a Catholic philosopher who was drawn into theology by the very logic of his understanding of what the intellectual life is. And the fact of the matter is that from a very early period Maritain, while recognizing the formal distinction between philosophy and theology, refused to permit them to be separate in his own life. One thinks of his contributions to the controversy over the concept of Christian philosophy. Like Edith Stein, in *Finite and Infinite Being*, and like his master, Maritain wants to present a synthesis which inevitably includes both philosophy and theology.

The insistence on the relevance of prayer for the intellectual life was an insistence on the existential setting in which thought takes place. To forget the real human condition, to forget that the philosopher is a man of flesh and bone, is to run the risk of becoming the comic figure of the practitioner of "Pure Thought" who was the object of Kierkegaard's mirth.

To call attention to the *personal* existential setting in which thinking occurs prepares for the *social* setting: *Le philosophe dans la cite*. This is not really an option. Contemplative withdrawal must be motivated by charity, and charity relates one to all men. The philosopher does not choose to be *dans la cite*, but he can choose the mode and degree of that involvement. Subsequent essays will draw attention to various aspects of Maritain's own social and political involvement. In this opening essay, I have wanted to suggest, however inadequately, the way in which there is fundamental continuity between, say, *La vie d'oraison* and *Humanisme integral*.

TWO

MARITAIN IN AND ON AMERICA

We Americans are embarrassingly eager to be instructed by others and there is ever a fresh supply of visiting pundits, condescending continentals and ideological intelligenstia to supply our need. Nowadays the United Nations has become a running seminar where diplomats from various totalitarian and/or undeveloped societies instruct us in our duties. And we pay for the privilege. I leave it to historians to determine if there has ever been docility such as ours since the beginning of recorded time.

In earlier, more leisurely eras, a book of reminiscences on America was a mandatory addition to a visiting European's *oeuvre* -- once he was safely home. Mrs. Trollope made a fortune with a book telling of her adventures among the wild Americans during her ill-fated effort to found an emporium in Cincinatti.

Dickens's *Notes on America* were more gentle, but still critical. He particularly disliked the spitting of tobacco juice. Anthony Trollope and Thackeray -- not to mention Oscar Wilde -- were more positive. In our own time, the negative British estimate of the United States has been carried on by Graham Greene.

All this by way of preface to some remarks about Jacques Maritain's reflections on America -- those contained in the 1958 book of that title, and those which antedate and follow it. Maritain himself refers to Chateaubriand and Tocqueville and we are at once put in mind of a French tradition in the literary genre referred to whose contributions are of a much more cerebral kind. Books 6 through 8 of *Memoires d'Outre-Tombe* tell of Chateaubriand's youthful visit to these shores and include his charming account of dropping by Washington's house in Philadelphia and being asked to come back for dinner. His comparison of Washington and Napoleon is striking: Washington, having helped lift his country to independence, died among the universal grief of his compatriots. Napoleon robbed France of independence, died in exile and the posted notice of his death was ignored by passersby. Like Tocqueville, Chateaubriand had come here to see the future and found that it worked. What failed in France, still flourished here. One gifted with a strong historical imagination can visualize the scene that met those friendly, intelligent and aristocratic eyes. America represented a political culture which, whatever its faults, was the future.

It was perfectly fitting that Maritain should cite these predecessors -- like theirs, his admiration for this country had profound roots. If democracy is the best political expression of Christianity, as Maritain held, and if democracy has achieved its highest level in the United States, as he also held, his interest had to be as intense as it was.

And yet his love for America surprised him. He had nursed the European prejudices he cites at the beginning of *Reflections on America*. In *Humanisme Integral* (1936), he sketched a political ideal which could only follow on the liquidation of capitalism. The latter book, incidentally, appeared three years after Maritain's first visit to the United States so that, if he speaks of love at first sight in 1957, a love which hits one "because he is confronted with a moral personality, a moral vocation, something of invaluable dignity, which is spiritual in nature, and which, I think, in the last analysis is quickened, in one way or another, by some spark of the Christian spirit and legacy," there may be some secondsight in his rememberance of his first sight. Nonetheless, the way Maritain describes the America to which he responded with love can serve as my text.

Maritain in America

Jacques Maritain's first visit to North America was in 1933 when he was asked to give a course at the Pontifical Institute of Mediaeval Studies at Toronto. From Toronto, he went to Chicago, where he lectured on "Culture and Liberty" in English, a language he claims he did not then know. Robert Hutchins, Mortimer Adler, John U. Nef -- friendships were made on that occasion that lasted a lifetime. Unsuccessful efforts were made to get Jacques an appointment at the University of Chicago, but he returned to give some lectures in the autumn of 1934. The visits to Chicago were repeated in 1938 and in 1940, when Jacques brought with him his wife Raissa and his sister-in-law

Vera Oumansoff. During the early Thirties, Maritain also began his connection with the University of Notre Dame where his friend Yves Simon was to teach before joining the faculty of the University of Chicago. Waldemar Gurian, founder of Notre Dame's *Review of Politics*, was involved in arrangements for Maritain's course on social and political philosophy given in South Bend in 1938. On this occasion, Maritain's anti-Franco stand called forth some sharp questioning, but this did not prevent the beginning of a long and almost sentimental association. Maritain was present for the opening of the Jacques Maritain Center in 1957 -- a photograph of the then aging philosopher, flanked by Joseph Evans, the first director of the Center, Father Leo R. Ward, C.S.C and Frank Keegan, commemorates the event -- and he actually bequeathed his heart to Notre Dame, but French medical laws prevented this wish from being carried out.

You will see that Maritain's first encounters with the United States were in the midwest. Nonetheless. He spoke in New York in 1934 -- where, along with academic and cultural notables, he came to know Dorothy Day and the Catholic Worker Movement -- and he lectured in Washington at the Catholic University of America. Thereafter, on his way to Toronto, as in 1938, he would spend some time in New York. He met the staff of *The Commonweal* and that was to be another long association; he also met Thomas Merton at this time. They were to be lifelong friends and among the most moving photographs John Howard Griffin took were those of Jacques and Merton in the latter's hermitage at Gethsemani Trappist Abbey in Kentucky.

In January, 1940, Maritain, his wife and his sister-in-law, sailed from France for what was to be a five year war time exile in the United States. The Maritains lived in New York and Jacques was involved in the Ecole Libre which was housed in the New School.

He continued to lecture at various universities -- Columbia, Princeton, Chicago, Notre Dame, Toronto -- as well as to give courses at the Ecole Libre. And he wrote. Late in 1944 he made a flying trip to France. The American sojourn ended in 1945 when Maritain was appointed French Ambassador to the Vatican.

Three years later, Maritain was offered and accepted an appointment to Princeton University, where he taught Thomistic moral philosophy for five years, from 1948 to 1952, after which he was given emeritus status. The Maritains continued to live in Princeton until 1960 when Jacques took his dying wife back to France. During this period, Maritain continued to teach and lecture at various universities -- the Walgreen lectures at the University of Chicago became *Man and the State*.

After the death of his wife, Maritain continued to make visits to the United States, coming to lecture at the old and favored places -- Notre Dame, Chicago, Toronto.

But enough. It is clear that Jacques Maritain was more than a visitor to the United States. From 1940 to 1960, with a three year hitch as Ambassador to the Vatican, he was resident in this country. Those two decades had been preceded by many visits, they would be followed by others. Maritain's contacts were many and various. When he spoke of this country, then, he did so with unusual authority. What did he have to say?

Maritain on America

I do not propose to present the full scope of Maritain's *Reflections on America*. For one thing, such a summary would suggest that the book itself is difficult, or large, or in need of some intermediary. It is none of these. It is a short book that speaks with immediacy to the reader, retaining the conversational tone of the three lectures to the Committee on Social Thought at the University of Chicago which form the basis of the book. I wish only to draw your attention to one or two items of random curiosity and then to concentrate on what seems to me essential to Maritain's vision of America.

One who reads this 1958 book some thirty years later will, I think, be struck by the absence of any reference to the atomic bomb or nuclear weapons. It has become fashionable to say that our minds have been haunted by thoughts of imminent annihilation since 1945. It is nice to have one's own memories corroborated by this silence in Maritain's reflections.

One is also struck by an untroubled certainty that democracy is not only the essence of America but that it is as well the future of the globe. These lectures were given during Eisenhower's second term, Adlai Stevenson is quoted in them, in a few years Kennedy's inaugural would give eloquent voice to the country's sense of an international mission. Maritain is clearly at home with this vision. How distant we seem today from that untroubled confidence, forever reading sinister motives into the almost missionary internationalism that then characterized the two national parties.

Again, one is struck by Maritain's remarks about capitalism. Among Maritain's first impressions of the country, he notes, was the sense that there is a conflict between the inner logic of capitalism and the people he saw living it. What is that inner logic? "Its inner logic, as I knew it -- originally grounded as it was on the principle of the fecundity of money and the absolute primacy of individual profit -- was, everywhere in the world, inhuman and materialist." This was the way he had envisaged capitalism in *Integral Humanism*. "But by a strange paradox, the people who lived and toiled under this structure or ritual of civilization were keeping their own souls apart from it. At least as regards the essentials, their souls and vital energy, their dreams, their everyday effort, their idealism and generosity, were running against the grain of the inner logic of the superimposed structure. They were freedom-loving and mankind-loving people, people clinging to the importance of ethical standards, anxious to save the world, the most humane and the least materialist among modern peoples which had reached the industrial stage." He returned to this in his sixth chapter, "The Old Tag of American Materialism," in which he develops at some length his conviction that we are not a materialist nation. Americans may be middle-class, but they are not bourgeois, not stingy, avaricious, narrowly possessive.

Well, all that makes pretty bracing reading, and it leads to what I regard as central to Maritain's notion of what America is. If we are not materialist, are we spiritual? Not only are we that, Maritain maintained that there is in this country a great thirst for, a great potential for -- contemplation. He mentions the popularity of the writings of Thomas Merton. He cites his own judgment of 1938 that a small but effective turn to contemplative activity will gradually "modify the general scheme of values." Characteristically, Maritain illustrates what he means by invoking American literature. "Let me only add that from *Moby Dick* and *The Scarlet Letter* to *Look Homeward, Angel* and *Requiem for a Nun* -- from Edgar Allan Poe and Emily Dickinson to Hart Crane, Allan Tate and T. S. Eliot (who has remained an American in spite of himself) -- American literature, in its most objectively careful scrutinies, has been preoccupied with the beyond and the nameless which haunt our blood. Man, as it sees him, is a restless being gropingly, sometimes miserably, at grips with his fleshly condition -- whom obviously no kind of materialist paradise can ever satisfy."

Three decades ago, we were seen by this astute visitor as a people with a spiritual destiny, a people whose literature, whose political structures, whose economy, revealed this orientation to the "something more," if not in actual fact, then in proximte potency.

These last remarks occur in a section late in *Reflections* in which Maritian makes explicit reference to the views he had expressed in *Integral Humanism*. There he had put forth an ideal of society as personalist, communitarian and pluralist. That society would be, not a sacral, but a secular one. What then of religion in America? In what way can the United States manifest the following notion? "One of the main themes in *Humanisme Integral* is the notion of a temporal civilization which is not 'sacral' but secular in nature, and in which men belonging to diverse spiritual lineages work together for the terrestial common good, but which, for all that, is a civilization religiously inspired and vitally Christian in its concrete behavior and morality as a social body." Maritain quotes an article by Peter Drucker in *The Review of Politics* (July, 1956) entitled "Organized Religion and the American Creed." Speaking of the "establishment clause" in the First Amendment, Drucker takes it to mean that the state must neither support nor favor any one religious denomination. "But at the same time the state must always sponsor, protect, and favor religious life in general. The United States is indeed a 'secular' state as faras any one denomination is concerned. But it is at the same time a 'religious' commonwealth as concerns the general belief in the necessity of a truly religious basis of citizenship." By citing this, Maritain accepts it as a gloss on what he means by a secular as opposed to a sacral society. Moreover, he quotes the following description of the Constitution from *Man and the State*: "It can be described as an outstanding lay Christian document tinged with the philosophy of the day. The spirit and inspiration of this great political Christian document is basically repugnant to the idea of making human society stand aloof from God and from any religious faith. Thanksgiving and public prayer, the invocation of the name of God at the occasion of any major official gathering, are, in the practical behavior of the nation, a token of this same spirit and inspiration." He sees the thought of the Founding Fathers, "their philosophy of life and their political philosophy, their notion of natural law and of human rights" permeated with concepts "worked out by Christian reason and backed up by an unshakable religious feeling."

What strange reading these thoughtful remarks make just thirty years after they were spoken. I propose to reflect on them in the light of recent national experience.

The Wider Context

The student of Maritain will realize that these reflections on America repose on a vast amount of writing about religion and politics in the modern state. One can speak without exagerration of Maritain's political philosophy but then one can also speak of his aesthetics, his philosophy of history and of science, his metaphysics, his account of contemplation. Maritain is a philosopher in the grand manner, of the old school; he is a systematic philosopher, not in the sense of professing a seamless whole closed in upon itself where every question has its answer. He is a Thomist, a student of St.

Thomas from the time of his conversion. This inspiration -- *Vae mihi si non thomistizavero,* he has exclaimed -- opened his mind to the full range of practical and theoretical questions and his published work makes it clear that he considered no part of knowledge and culture alien to him. Now, the importance of this for understanding his political views is clear. His ultimate perspective will be, if not overtly theological, then metaphysical, and by that I mean theistic.

For the Thomist, man acts for an end because he is part of a teleological cosmos. Purpose is not confined to the human realm but permeates the natural world as well. This by contrast to discussion of morals and politics which assume that the natural world -- and this includes the human body -- is the realm of necessity, pushed from behind, not tugged forward by a goal, whereas man with his projects is superimposed on this inert background. How can freedom blend with such necessity? For Maritain, the world and man have destinies, from God they come, to God they go. If this is the case, then an atheistic account must be wrong.

It will be seen that this is almost precisely the opposite outlook from that which seems dominant now. The current working assumption is that our view of man and society must be godless, at most neutral toward theism, in practise antagonistic to it. The citizen who thinks his religious beliefs are relevant to political action is regarded as a menace, one who would impose his private beliefs -- false, of course -- on his fellows. If he would function in civil society, he must become for the nonce an agnostic, a believer for whom his religious beliefs are irrelevant. Is not this the prominent understanding of the separation of Church and State, so much so that it is espoused and preached by Catholic politicians? Is this not why we find it almost quaint for Maritain, and Peter Drucker, to say that while the state must espouse no one denomination, it must promote religion? From the latter day point of view, Maritain's vision of the secular state lookds decidedly sacral.

Democracy as a Faith

One of the most astonishing aspects of Maritain's political theory is the use to which he puts the Augustinian distinction between the City of God and the City of Man. What he calls a sacral society is a state or political community which smudges the difference between the two cities. This fusion was possible in times when there was a religious faith common to all citizens, but in modern times, where a diversity of faiths and indeed the presence of atheists within the political community are commonplace, such a sacral approach is no longer possible.

It must not be thought that Maritain regards the gradual separation of the spiritual and temporal as a declension, as a failure of Christianity. *Au contraire*. Or at least, not quite. This separation is a result of a "process which was in itself but a development of the Gospel distinction between the things that are Caesar's and the things that are God's -- the civil society has become grounded on a common good and a common task which are of an earthly, 'temporal' or 'secular' order, and in which citizens belonging to diverse spiritual groups or lineages share equally. Religious division among men is in itself a misfortune. But it is a fact that we must will-nilly recognize." In the temporal order, however, democracy can play a role analogous to that faith plays in the religious realm. Maritain does not

hesitate to speak of "the democratic secular faith." " A
genuine democracy implies a fundamental agreement
between minds and wills on the bases of life in common;
it is aware of itself and of its principles, and it must be
capable of defending and promoting its own conception
of social and political life; it must bear within itself a
common human creed, the creed of freedom." He
contrasts this with bourgeois liberal democracy of the
19th century that imagined that it could accomodate
conceptions inimical to its own foundations, that it
could be "neutral even with regard to freedom."   It
lacked a common good, it had no real common thought,
it produced a society with no common faith. "The faith
in question is a *civic* or *secular* faith, not a religious one."
Not only is this faith not a rival to religious faith,
according to Maritain, the more lively the religious faith,
the more deeply would the secular faith in the
democractic charter be adhered to. The reason for this is
simply that democracy itself has sprung from a
Christian inspiration, it is a political expression of the
Gospel.

Martiain is not through with the analogy. If faith, then
heretics. There are, he says, political heretics who work
to destroy the bases of common life, which bases are
freedom and the practical secular faith expressed in the
democratic charter.

I draw attention to these few facets of Chapter V of
Man and the State because they are clearly what
underpins Maritain's views toward this country in
Reflections on America. Those few remarks at the end of
the latter work which suggest that, much to Maritain's
own surprise, the United States is close to the ideal he
sketched in *Humanisme Integral*, are seriously meant.

Here is a sort of sorites expressing Maritain's outlook:

Maritain was a Roman Catholic with an unshakeable
faith in the truth of Christianity.

If Christianity is true, then what it says of man and human destiny is also true.

The freedom and dignity of the person are central to the faith and these tenets have fostered a gradual evolution of political thought and institutions in the direction of democracy.

But democratic faith in free cooperation need not be grounded on Christian faith -- the very Christian distinction between God and Caesar asserts this.

That is why, despite the talk of the democratic faith and political heretics, Maritian considers the democratic charter to be productive of a secular rather than a sacral society.

Moreover, despite the conflicting justifications that may be offered for the democractic charter -- the democratic faith is, he holds, a matter of practical rather than theoretical agreement -- there is a sense in which this does not matter. There is implicitly present in this faith its true foundation, no matter the false theories that might be constructed.

The secular foundation of the democratic faith is natural law.

In that sequence, we have, I believe, the nub of Maritain's thought about democracy. And, of course, the retort will be that Natural Law is every bit as problematical to the "modern mind" as Christian faith.

The Rights Of Man

What prepared Maritain's position on the democratic faith and its true foundation was his reflections on the notion of universal human rights. Chapter IV of *Man and the State* both recalls and completes his thoughts on this subject, and the lengthy title of the opening section is a statement of his fundamental thesis: *Men mutually opposed in their theoretical conceptions can come to a merely practical agreement regarding a list of human rights.* Maritain had before him not only the 18th century universal declaraction of human rights but also the International Declaration on Human Rights published by the United Nations in 1948. Indeed, he had been his country's delegate to the UNESCO meeting in Mexico City that fashioned this document. How was agreement on such a list possible between governments and socieites of such deeply divided ideas on man?

There is, of course, a cynical reply to that. Nor must we think Maritain is naive. Later in *Man and the State*, discussing world government, he notes that his basic Aristotelianism makes him wary of such a concept. It should also dictate wariness about international declarations on human rights. It will be noticed that Maritain insists that the agreement is not an agreement on the basis of those rights. "Yet it would be quite futile to look for a common *rational justification* of these practical conclusions and these rights." Nonetheless, rational justifications are necessary, indispensable, even though they are powerless to create agreement among men. "As long as there is no unity of faith or unity of philosophy in the minds of men, the interpretations and justifications will be in mutual conflict." The agreement, he maintains, is practical, even pragmatic, rather than theoretical.

Now Maritain holds that there is one true theoretical or philosophical foundation of human rights and that others are false or woefully inadequate. He thinks others have a theoretical or philosophical foundation and that, if it is in conflict with his own, it is false. Yet, from a practical point of view, this does not matter.

Surely this is a curious position, and if this were all there is to it, the obvious retort would be that the agreement Maritain speaks of is at most verbal. If "freedom of expression" or "freedom to emigrate" men quite different things in different societies, what is the value of "agreeing" on freedom of expression and freedom to emigrate? Unless Maritain can maintain that in some fundamental sense those who disagree are in agreement -- and not merely what he calls practical agreement -- his position must seem cynical. But of course Natural Law is a justification which includes the claim that everyone has the wherewithal right now to see the truth of that justification. This is the point of introducing here his distinction between the ontological natural law and the gnoseological natural law, the former being the real basis for the latter recognition.

Natural Law theory maintains that even those who reject it are accepting it, at least to some degree, and the degree to which they accept it is the seed of theoretical and not merely practical agreement. The ontological natural law is therefore the implicit and often unrecognized basis for the kind of practical agreement Maritain speaks of, and it can ground a theoretical agreement as well when the ground (the ontological) is know (the gnoselelogical). As St. Thomas insisted, it is very much like saying that one who denies the principle of contradiction must invoke it; so too, one who denies the precepts of natural law nonetheless implicitly honors them.

Concluding

Jacques Maritain joins a long list of Frenchmen who saw beneath the surface roughness of this country , beneath its flaws and imperfections, a universal human ideal being realized. When his earlier more or less standard anti-Americanism and anti-capitalism evaporated because of a lenghty sojourn here, he did not need to concoct a new theory to explain his affection and respect for the United States. Rather, it seemed to him that, though he had not suspected it before, this country best exemplified a democractic ideal he had been trying to formulate earlier. His experience here did not generate a new theory. Rather familiarity with America led him to think that we met the specifications of a theory he had already formed. This is not said to diminish the very real love he felt for America. Who has not felt that his beloved assumes a waiting role even as she shapes and alters it?

THREE

REFLECTIONS ON CHRISTIAN PHILOSOPHY

It is not without significance for the theme of our
meeting that, in a chapter entitled "Christian
Philosophy" in his remarkable memoir, *The Philosopher
and Theology*, Etienne Gilson discussed the encyclical
Aeterni Patris, drawing attention to what became the
traditional way of referring to it, viz. "On the
Restoration in Catholic Schools of Christian Philosophy
According to the Mind of the Angelic Doctor Saint
Thomas Aquinas." Any discussion of the development
of Gilson's thought and his altering interpretation of the
writings of Saint Thomas, which can be traced through
the various editions of *Le Thomisme*, must, I think, take
into account the effect on him of the quarrel about the
very concept of Christian Philosophy which began in
1931 and continued for some years, largely in France,
and came to include many of the great figures of
contemporary French philosophy, Gilson himself, Emile
Brehier who in effect began the quarrel, Jacques

Maritain, Leon Brunschvicg, Van Steenberghen, Noel, Blondel and Renard, to name only the chief figures. That quarrel is discussed by Maurice Nedoncelle in his *Is There a Christian Philosophy?* and Andre Henry in " La querelle de la philosophie chretienne: histoire et bilan d'un debat."

I do not propose to trace the outlines of that famous discussion here, nor to discuss the various works in which Gilson returned to the question and sharpened his own position, works like *Christianisme et Philosophie* in 1949 and *Introduction a la Philosophie Chretienne* in 1960, to say nothing of the master work *The Spirit of Mediaeval Philosophy*, the Gifford Lectures delivered in 1931-1932 when the controversy had hardly begun. The problem of Christian Philosophy pervades the work of Gilson after 1931 and nothing less than a detailed and circumstantial discussion of his *oeuvre* could possibly do justice to his views. my intention here is far more modest.

I shall content myself with a number of *obiter dicta* on a distinction made by Jacques Maritain in his little book *De la philosophie chretienne*, published in 1933, and then go on to say a few things about the present status of Christian Philosophy in the United States.

Matters having to do with the adjective in the phrase "Christian Philosophy" were, Maritain felt, better discussed with reference to the *state* of philosophy rather than its *nature*. Thus, to ask about the present status of Christian Philosophy is seemingly to embark upon an infinite regress -- the state of the state, etc. Of course there is no real ambiguity here. Only a philosopher would have trouble with the wording of my task. Having proved that, if only glancingly, I pass on to the topic itself.

In the early Thirties, when Gilson and Maritain responded to the querilous claim of Brehier that the concept of Christian Philosophy was incoherent, they quickly and rightly turned from Brehier's pseudo-problem to issues that were their own and more important. The swiftest response to the charge was, *circumspice*, look around you. The Middle Ages provide us with numerous instances of Christian Philosophy. *Ab esse ad posse valet illatio. Ergo*, etc. Neither Maritain nor Gilson let it go at that, needless to say. Clearly the charge stirred up in them a desire to reflect on what they were doing as philosophers who were Catholics. I want to recall very briefly what I take to be the abiding significance of what they had to say -- it is because it is abiding that it fits under the title of our symposium -- and then to go on to characterize the philosophizing of Catholics in the United States today, with an added reference to the Society of Christian Philosophers formed just a few years ago.

The discussion of Christian Philosophy in the work of Maritain mentioned above moves on two levels, what I will call the modal and the substantive levels.

Indiquons tout de suite quel est pour nous le principe de la solution; c'est la distinction classique entre *l'ordre de specification* et *l'ordre d'exercise*, ou encore, et c'est a ces termes que nous nous tiendrons, entre la nature et l'etat.

The modal level is captured by the distinction between nature and state, nature and condition, the order of specification and the order of exercise. It is not necessary to think of philosophy as some inert nature having properties of its own which is then carried around by various sweating Atlases whose itinerary is the basis for a number of *per accidens* remarks about their burden. Better to think of the activity of philosophizing -- *philosophieren*, as Pieper puts it -- and to distinguish what characterizes it formally as such from what characterizes it as undertaken by so-and-so in such-and-such circumstances.

It is easy for us to see the kind of distinction involved in the case of the moral appraisal of a given act of thinking or philosophizing. The act of thinking is good if it achieves its end which is truth. But the act, thus appraised, may be appraised differently, and negatively, because of the circumstances in which it takes place. If I am lolling on my yacht devising sound and convincing proofs for the existence of God while ignoring cries for help from drowning swimmers, it is clear that my thinking may receive a plus or a minus depending on our point of view. A judgement of the content of thought as opposed to a judgement of the engagement in thinking by this concrete person here and now, that is the distinction. Of course, it would be odd and otiose to respond to the statement "Whatever is moved is moved by another" by asking "When? In the morning or evening? In the Northern Hemisphere as well as the Southern?" By the same token the schoolyard response, "Who says so?" would be inappropriate. We might, of course, want to make a similar distinction between sentences like "Roses are red" and "I have a toothache," saying that the latter but not the former involves the reporter in the report and thus is differently appraised with regard to its truth. But the distinction I am after is one that would distinguish the intrinsic judgement of an act of thinking (true or false?) from the moral judgement of it (good or bad?).

For an act of thinking to be true is for it to be good in one sense, but not in the moral sense. Just as it is not necessarily appropriate to utter any truth in just any circumstances (to do so would be a sign of madness, gaucherie or breach of promise among other things), so the appraisal of an act of thinking as true is not the end of the matter. Even remarks about roses are said by someone in particular circumstances and while we may agree that roses are red and violets are blue, that does not settle whether the person uttering these simple truths is engaged in wooing, translating from the Portuguese, encoding security information for the enemy, talking in his sleep or composing a valentine that Hallmark will not buy.

It is best to make the distinction where there is conflict, but of course it can happen that the act of thinking is approved on both levels. The classical conception of philosophy presupposed that even theoretical thinking would be, as well as the attainment of truth, a morally good activity. Indeed, one adumbration of the problem of Christian Philosophy in antiquity is the question as to whether a bad man could be a good philosopher, that is, the role of ethics in the philosophical life and the description of the philosophical ideal. It went without saying that the good ruler had to be a good man. How far have we come from that classical conception, even in the practical realm.

My suggestion, then, is that we can approach one facet of Maritain's handling of the question of Christian Philosophy by seeing the difference between a moral and an intrinsic appraisal of an act of theoretical thinking. Once we remind ourselves that the truth can be sought out of motives of vanity or the will to power or to *eparter la bourgeoisie*, we can see how one might want so to describe the philosophical ideal as to insist that the right deed be done for the right reason and to suggest that without the proper moral orientation the whole thing is worthless. Plato held that it is moral virtue which gives us that necessary affinity with the really real which enables knowledge to take place. The elaboration of this *pathein/mathein* view lifts the moral from mere modal status to a substantive feature of philosophizing.

One of the curiosities of the debate on Christian Philosophy that should not go unremarked, was the tendency of those who cast themselves in the role of defending *pure* philosophy is a rich subject for comedy and no one had more fun with it than Kierkegaard. Pure Thought is thought without a thinker, and philosophers began to think of themselves as identified with that abstraction. Unamuno, somewhat lugubriously, makes a similar point in *The Tragic Sense of Life* when he speaks of the man of flesh and bones. But of course theoretical thinking is merely one of the activities a man may engage in; not only can he not devote himself exclusively to it, in the life of even the most dedicated scholar it amounts to a small portion of his day. Getting from A to B, opening and shutting doors, lighting one's pipe, deciding to read this book or that, to write or think some more, on and on. There is a whole quotidian network that surrounds intellectual activity and without which it cannot be understood. That network includes implicit and explicit certainties about the world and ourselves and this has the quite unsurprising implication, save for some philosophers, that we *bring* truths to our philosophizing; not all knowledge is the *result* of philosophizing.

Needless to say, taking the quotidian network into account casts into an appropriately hilarious light the notion that philosophy should begin with doubt.

When philosophers have managed to expunge such home truths from their minds, they have fashioned wrong and dangerous conceptions of man. Thus, if one equates being a man, being human, with engaging in theoretical thinking of the most abstract kind, say, geometry, it would seem to follow from the fact that not even geometers do geometry most of the time that few men ever engage in the supposed specifically human activity. But what is to be said of all those activities humans engage in if they cannot be called human? Out of this exiguous picture of man came, inevitably, the bloodless moral philosophy we are only now beginning to free ourselves from.

It is only when everyone engaged in the discussion stops talking about *pure philosophy*, in the sense of thought without a thinker, that it is possible to ask what is *peculiar* about what the Christian brings to the activity of philosophizing and how it differs from what others, e.g. secular humanists, bring to the task. One of the peculiarities of the Roman Catholic philosopher, as witness this symposium, is that he takes with the utmost seriousness documents emanating from Rome and having to do with his activity, documents like the encyclical *Aeterni Patris*.

Docility to the Ordinary Magisterium has fallen on bad days, of course, with the theologians seemingly eager to quibble with, distance themselves from or outrightly oppose Christ's vicar on earth. I prefer to direct my incredulity at such theologians and to rejoice in the fact that the Church has consistently and over many centuries put before the Catholic intellectual, particularly the philosopher and theologian, Saint Thomas Aquinas as a model. *Vae mihi si non Thomistizavero*, Maritain wrote, and we might render it: For me not to follow Saint Thomas would be my ruin. That is the attitude we hope to see embodied in the Center whose inauguration we are celebrating. Anyone who thinks of that ideal as narrow or constraining need only consider the works of Etienne Gilson and Jacques Maritain. It was not merely one pope or one council or one committee that recommended Saint Thomas to us as a guide; it is the consistent and reiterated message of the Ordinary Magisterium. The only appropriate attitude toward this undeniable fact on the part of the Catholic is to see it as meant to help him attain the objectives of philosophy and theology. *Gustate et videte.*

This has to do with the starting point of our philosophizing. With what author should we begin? Any neophyte begins somewhere. why does he begin where he does? The particular answers to that would be as numerous as the beginners but it seems fair enough to bring them all under one umbrella: one begins the study of philosophy where he does because he trusts someone. That is the common condition of the student. Viewed in this light, the situation of the Catholic is like anyone else's. But, of course, when he considers the authority and trustworthiness of *his* advisor, he can only conclude that he is in a far better position.

It is time that the Catholic intellectual resist the view that his existential situation is anomolous and in need of apology and adopt the more seemly stance of being grateful for the guidance he receives from the Church. The gift of faith is the best thing that ever happened to the human mind and the counsel and advice of those in whose keeping the deposit of faith is entrusted should be welcomed and received with joy, a joy which will eventually become a *gaudium de veritate*. It is silly to think that the upshot of all Catholics taking this advice will be uniformity and homogeneity of thinking. There is a single moral ideal for human persons which, if we pursue it seriously, will lead to a far greater differentiation among us rather than to somber sameness.

In the past several decades, interest in the thought of Saint Thomas has waned among Catholics even as it has waxed among our separated brethren. Doubtless there are dozens of reasons for this, few of them praiseworthy. Let us hope that the Center for Thomistic Studies here at the University of Saint Thomas will be a harbinger of a new renaissance of Thomism. Let us take up our all but discarded patrimony again and try to establish a mood like that which animated Etienne Gilson, Jacques Maritain, Charles De Koninck and Yves

Simon, to speak only of those who came from abroad. Oh for the exuberance of a Chesterton, quoted to such effect by Pope John XXIII when he opened the Second Vatican Council! Those of us who have only fitfully and inadequately allowed our philosophizing to be guided by St. Thomas Aquinas no longer merely believe that he is a good guide. It is something we have come to know. And that of course is the justification of the guidance. *Oportet addiscentem credere.* The complement of that truth is that, *in philosophy,* authority is the weakest argument.

So too Maritain, having provided a modal religious context within which philosophical thinking takes place, goes on to suggest that the objects of religious faith, believed truths, exercise an intrinsic influence on philosophical content, on philosophical; truth. He does not want to say that the origin of a philosophical truth in a revealed truth -- he takes creation as an example -- means that the acceptance of this truth is always and everywhere dependent upon religious belief.

A few years ago we formed the Society of Christian Philosophers, a group that holds regional meetings -- these have been held at the University of Notre Dame as well as at Wheaton College in Illinois -- and national meetings in conjunction with the eastern meeting of the American Philosophical Association.

It is a welcome thing to have philosophers identify themselves as Christians and, by doing so, to suggest that this has significance for them as philosophers. By and large, the non-Catholic membership in the Society consists of Evangelicals and Calvinists and Lutherans. Not surprisingly, when one considers the dominant themes of recent Philosophy of Religion, a central theme of the society is that religious belief is rational, a reasonable activity to engage in. What I want to draw attention to, by way of contrast to what such a claim would mean in the context of *Aeterni Patris*, is the minimalistic, not to say fideistic, flavor of the thought of many of my colleagues in the Society.

If one maintains that belief is reasonable in the sense that no one can successfully convict the believer of inconsistency, contradiction, or some other mode of irrationality, this is nothing. Oftentimes this position takes the form of a So's your old man argument. A classical instance of this can be found in Alvin Plantinga's *God and Other Minds*. The upshot of the book is that it is no less reasonable to assert the existence of God than it is to assert the existence of other minds. This does not come down to any direct assertion that it is reasonable to affirm the existence of God. The technique of the book has led to the neologism "to alvinize." One alvinizes when, confronted by an attack on religious belief, one responds by seeking and finding a tenet of the attacker that can be shown to be at least as suspect, on the attacker's grounds, as the claims of religious belief. The *tu quoque* or *ad hominem* flavor of this is at once its appeal and its limitation.

In the same book, Plantinga examines versions of traditional proofs for the existence of God and finds them wanting. The suggestion thus is that while nothing positive can be rationally established with respect to theism, insofar as theism has problems they are shared by many convictions that the atheist (Plantinga's atheologist) would be most reluctant to relinquish.

If Plantinga is typical of the Society -- a pleasant thought since he is one of the most gifted philosophers and one of the most edifying Calvinists I know -- it would be fair to say that fideism is rampant in the Society of Christian Philosophers. The status of Christian Philosophy should be discussed, I think, with particular reference to the status of natural theology.

Traditionally understood, the reasonableness of belief is a claim that has reposed on an interpretation of Romans 1:19-20 which has it that men capable, independently, of faith, of arriving at knowledge of the invisible things of God. This is a task which cannot be ignored. Techniques such as alvinizing are useful and good and we should be grateful for them. But to settle for them would be to abandon one of the essential features of Christian Philosophy, viz. that there are sound and valid proofs of God's existence and of other *praeambula fidei* and that this provides a basis for the argument that it is reasonable to accept the *mysteria fidei* as true.

At the risk of unction of the extremer sort, let me conclude by drawing attention to a little book that Maritain authored with his wife Raissa, *Prayer and Intelligence*. As in Maritain's greatest work, *Les degres du savoir*, the smaller work, originally titled *La vie d'Oraison*, reminds us that just as the ethical provides a wider context in which the activity of theoretical thinking can be appraised, so too does religion. God did not become man in order that men might become theologians. Contemplation, the fulfillment of the spiritual life, is the common supernatural goal of human persons. It is no less the goal of the Christian Philosopher. Just as there has been an unhappy dissociation of thought of thought and life, so there can be in the believer a dissociation of thought and the spiritual life. Saint Thomas, we remember, began study with a prayer and his study thus became a species of prayer. It is not without significance that the patron of Catholic intellectual life is a saint. Bloy's adage still obtains. There is only one tragedy, not to become a saint. How many saintly philosophers do you know? That is a judgement on us. The deepest significance of the notion of Christian Philosophy is that it would have us avoid a tragic life in this sense.

FOUR

THE GOD OF THE PHILOSOPHERS

The God of the philosophers, Pascal remarked, is not the God of Abraham and Isaac, and of course he meant something by it a good deal more divisive than I might mean by saying that the God of Pascal is not the God of Paul Claudel. Nor would the contrast be the same if Pascal were separating Abraham and Isaac from those *cuius deus venter est.* Pascal is calling our attention in a dramatic way to the contrast of faith and reason. Perhaps the contrast is in itself dramatic whether it be found with its *relata* located in different persons or in the same human breast. Certainly it provided intellectual drama of a high order in the 13th Century when the Christian West was suddenly confronted with an influx of philosophical literature, Greek and Arabic, which dealt in novel and, as it seemed to many, threatening ways of fundamental theological matters.

Those of us living now, beneficiaries of the two great Vatican Councils, may pardonably feel that whatever

difficulties might attend the relations of faith and reason
have long since been sorted out. After all, we can read
the following in the Dogmatic Constitution Dei Filius,
on Faith, of Vatican I:

> Hoc quoque perpetuus Ecclesiae catholicae consensus
> tenuit et tenet, duplicam esse ordinem cognitionis non
> solum principio, sed obiecto etiam distinctum: principio
> quidem, quia in altero naturali ratione, in altero fid
> divina cognoscimus; obiecto autem, quia praeter ea, ad
> quae naturalis ratio pertingere potest, credenda nobis
> proponuntur mysteria in Deo abscondita, quae, nisi
> revelata divinitus, innotescere non possunt. Quocirca
> Apostolus, qui a gentibus Deum 'per ea, quae facta sunt'
> (Rom I.20) cognitum esse testatur, disserens tamen de
> gratia et veritate, quae 'per Jesum Christum facta est'
> (cf Io 1.17), pronuntiat: 'Loquimur Dei sapientiam in
> mysterio, quae abscondita est, quam praedestinavit
> Deus ante saecula in gloriam nostram, quam nemo
> principum huius saeculi cognovit ... nobis autem
> revelavit Deus per spiritum suum.... (Denz. 3015)

Faith and reason, coming from the same divine
source, cannot conflict and the believer who accepts
truths on the basis of God revealing can be confident
that they will not conflict with truths gained by
inquiring reason.

Well, things did not always look so clear. In what
follows I want to do two main things: (1) with particular
reference to the historical setting in which he worked, I
want to discuss what Thomas Aquinas made of the God
of the philosophers, and then (2) I want to take up the
point latent in the Pascalian phrase, discussing it *ad
mentem divi Thomas, ut ita dicam,* and say why it is that
we respond favorably to the suggestion that there is
something radically inadequate in philosophical proofs
of God's existence -- or if, not precisely inadequate ,
dissatisfying.

I

Let me begin with a reference to an early sixth century work on which Thomas Aquinas wrote an incomplete commentary, namely the *De trinitate* of Boethius. This wonderful little opusculum sets out to discuss a central Christian mystery in a way that will show the influence of St. Augustine's massive work of the same title: the Trinity of Persons in the divine nature. At the outset of Chapter 2, Boethius recalls for his reader that speculative science is divided into three kinds: physics, mathematics and theology. The distinction is Aristotelian and the way in which Boethius goes on to describe the objects of these three sciences owes a good deal to Aristotle's discussion in E.1 of the *Metaphysics*. As it happens, Thomas's commentary breaks off just after treating of the division of speculative philosophy and the mode of treatment appropriate to each branch of it.

What is particularly puzzling about Boethius's procedure is this: wishing to discuss a matter of Christian faith, a mystery, he introduces a division of intellectual labor borrowed from a pagan philosopher, with the suggestion that what Aristotle or, more generally, a philosopher, meant by theology indicates the area to which discussion of the Trinity belongs. That is surprising if only because of its suggestion that there is an effective identity of the God of the philosophers and the God of Christian belief. Whether or not Boethius really meant this suggestion is not a matter into which I intend to go here. In any case, he provided Thomas with an occasion to speak of two senses of the term "theology" with the possibility of allocating the philosophical discussion of God to theology in one of its senses and the Christian discussion of God to theology in the other of its senses.

In order to grasp what he has to say on this point, which is the chief one interesting us, we must at least allude to what Boethius and his commentator say here about what will formally characterize the subject matters of different theoretical sciences. For reasons which Thomas spells out at some length, it is the mode of defining which is the crucial point of reference, and the various ways in which the sciences exclude matter from the definitions of their objects is the formal basis of the plurality of speculative sciences.

Arcane matters, these, but in the case of what were for Aristotle non-problematical instances of science, namely physics and mathematics, easily enough grasped. The naturalist speaks of things defined in such a way that it is clear that they are subject to change and possess sensible qualities; mathematicals, on the other hand, are not thought of as heavy or light, smooth or rough, warm or cool. The mathematician is thus said to abstract from sensible qualities, to consider things without thinking of matter or sensible qualities. Do such things exist? Are there existent things which respond just as such to the considerations of the mathematician? Aristotle's answer to that, you know, was in the negative, and Thomas agreed with him.

Against that background, the possibility of a science beyond physics (and mathematics) can be expressed as one whose objects are defined without matter and which exist without matter. Metaphysics, theology, divine science, considers things which are both thought of without matter and which can exist without matter. The Greek term *theion* modified things which persist in being, which are not subject to change. A thing whose grasp on existence is easily lost is less of a being than one with a more tenacious grasp, and the best things of all, divine things, are those which cannot cease to be. You may question this hierarchy by citing the example of a persistent cold or pain to which a fleeting pleasure seems preferable. Of course it is. Disease is considered by the Greek to be a disorder, a lack, a want, and pain is a sign of its presence. Suffice it to say that the Greek thought of these difficulties and came up with ways to dismiss them as threats to the notion of a hierarchy of being.

The difficult question asks what reason we have to believe there are immaterial things. One can grant that, if there are such things, they are better than corruptible things, but that does not decide the issue. Aristotle's view, which Thomas followed, had it that it is not self-evident that there are immaterial things. If the statement that something immaterial exists is true, its truth must be established, proved, derived, from truths about material things. This is the very structure of proofs of God's existence.

The medievals did not have to await the late 12th Century in order to become aware of proofs for the existence of God. Early in that century, Anselm had fashioned a cosmological proof as well as his more famous ontological one, and there were proofs deriving from Augustine which purported to show that, given certain truths about the world, about creation, it follows that there must be a God. Perhaps it was because such proofs occurred in settings the believer found congenial that they did not disturb him or lead to dark thoughts about the God of the philosophers. You remember how reluctant Augustine was to allow that Plato could have taught the things he did without contact with the Jews, as if any truth about God must derive in some way from Revelation. The case of Boethius, already alluded to, is instructive. It is not really until the 13th Century that we find clearcut distinctions between philosophy and theology or, as is the case with Thomas, between philosophical and Scriptural theology.

In order to know that being and material being are not synonymous one must have a proof that there exists something immaterial. A proof for the existence of God attempts to show that given material things there must exist something else and that something else is God. What the proofs actually conclude to is that there is a first unmoved mover, or a first efficient or final cause, or some such descriptive phrase as those which is taken to refer to what the term God refers to.

How laborious all that must seem to one who has believed in God from his mother's knee. For such a one, God is a father, is incarnate in Jesus, made heaven and earth, and so on. These truths are not accepted against the background of any argument or sophisticated inquiry. That is the first contrast we notice between reason and faith, philosophy and faith, with respect to the conviction that there is a God.

But there was something far more than a difference in origin, as if some pagans proved that God exists while believers accept on the basis of Revelation, thanks to grace, that there is a God. Christians of the 13th Century, confronted with the philosophy of Aristotle, along with Islamic commentaries on it, came to hold, some of them, most notably St. Bonaventure, that the philosopher said *false* things about God, and that was the real difference. So it was not that the true things the philosopher says are based on argument rather than faith; the philosopher is uttering falsehoods which must be labeled as such.

It was the errors of Aristotle that Bonaventure insisted on: Aristotle held things which called into question personal immortality, divine providence and the creation of the world in time. Bonaventure was sure that Aristotle was teaching things which went contrary to the faith and that consequently Aristotle was wrong.

Let us pause for a moment at this initial result of the juxtaposition of faith and reason. If faith is the acceptance of certain matters as true, it follows that whatever stands in contradictory opposition to what is believed must be false. Two things are operative here: (a) that faith bears on the true and (b) the principle of contradiction. If the principle of contradiction is the basic ground of rationality or reasonableness, then the policy of the believer is eminently reasonable. For him to entertain the possibility that something which is contradictory to what he believes to be true might be true, would be an irrational policy.

That is why it would be wrong to deride St. Bonaventure. He is right as rain in his assumptions and Thomas Aquinas is in perfect agreement with him. Where the two men disagree is in their assessment of what Aristotle actually said. As it happens, Thomas denies that Aristotle teaches the things which are undoubtedly contrary to revealed truth and thus false. In the *De aeternitate mundi* Thomas argues that, while we know from revelation that the world had a beginning in time, the contradictory is, while false, not impossible. That is, Thomas does not think he can fashion an argument which would show that the world must necessarily have had a beginning time. And he does not think Aristotle thought he could show that. If then Aristotle is merely assuming that the world could have existed always, that is not in contradiction to the faith. (Later, in commenting on the *Physics*, Thomas somewhat alters his view of what Aristotle meant.)

In the *De unitate intellectus*, Thomas argues against the Averroists, that Aristotle means to say that the agent intellect is a faculty of each and every human soul and that, consequently, the proof for the incorruptibility of the human soul is a proof for the lastingness of my soul and yours and all human souls, that is, it is tantamount to a proof of personal immortality.

As for the assumption that Aristotle's definition of God as Thought thinking itself is incompatible with Providence, Thomas denies that this entails that God is not aware of all the things he causes.

Thomas clearly spent a good deal more time than Bonaventure in the effort to understand Aristotle. We have not a single Bonaventurean commentary on a work of Aristotle, whereas the *Opera omnia* of Aquinas contain more than a dozen such commentaries to say nothing of such occasional works as those just cited. Nor were these commentaries on Aristotle products of Thomas's tasks as a theologian. Nonetheless, one can say that his overall aim in poring over Aristotle was a theological one.

Thomas and Bonaventure are one in this, that if A is a truth of faith and some philosopher taught -A, we know immediately that -A is false. Thus far, we have Bonaventure and Aquinas disagreeing over whether Aristotle taught -A. Well, let us say that he did.

First, there is the inescapable fact that "God exists" is not only a truth philosophers attempt to prove, it is included among the things that have been revealed; indeed, one might say that it is implicit in every other truth God reveals. Very well. There is a truth which is numbered among the truths about God which can be proved, and which if Thomas is right has been proved by philosophers, but which is also numbered among the truths about Himself that God has revealed and which believers accept on that basis.

We might attempt to escape this by saying that "God exists" is not the conclusion of any historically formulated proof for the existence of God but that won't do. As is clear from each of the quinque viae of St. Thomas, the conclusion of the proof is taken to by synonymous with "God exists." Thus, after he has recounted the proof of the existence of a Prime Mover, Thomas adds, and this all men take to be God. God is described as the Prime Mover and is proved to exist *under that description.* Could we not then say that God is known under some descriptions and believed under others? And would we not then have a way of distinguishing the God of the philosophers from the God of religious belief?

As it happens, this is not a route Thomas Aquinas takes. He holds that God is known under descriptions which are identical to those we find in Revelation. That is, if the philosopher can prove that there is a first cause on which all else depends, and God is this first cause, the God of revelation is also the first cause of all else. How can Thomas hold both (1) that there are truths which are both known by philosophers and included in revelation and (2) that knowledge and faith are formally distinct.

It is quite clear that he holds a formal distinction between knowing something and believing something. A knowledge claim reposes on evidence, one *sees* that something is true; a belief claim reposes on authority, one holds something is true on someone's say so. But what is revealed is held on the authority of God revealing. It would seem then that Thomas cannot consistently hold that the same truth can be known and be revealed.

What Thomas does is to distinguish (a) what has been revealed and (b) what must be taken to be true on authority. Since the equivalent of "God exists" can be known and since "God exists" is included in Revelation, he concludes that Revelation includes at least some truths which can be known to be true quite apart from Revelation. Thus there is an overlap of knowledge and Revelation. But there is no overlap of knowledge and faith in the strict sense. This is why Thomas distinguishes revealed truths into Preambles of Faith and Mysteries of Faith. The mysteries of faith are those truths which can only be held to be true on the authority of God, e.g. the Trinity and Incarnation. The Preambles of Faith are revealed truths which we can come to know to be true. That there is a God, that He is one, that there cannot be several Gods, -- these are truths we believed from our mother's knee, but which can be established on the basis of sound argument.

The bulk of the truths about God which have been revealed are mysteries -- from first to last we hold them to be true on God's authority. One who believes A to be true may be certain that -A is false, but that does not mean he is in possession of an argument which shows -A to be false. And, unless one is believer, he is going to need some ground for saying that -A is false. This is why Bonaventure set out to show that it would have been *impossible* for the world always to have existed. His argument rests on the assumption that, if the world had always existed, there must now be some largest possible number, that is, a number to which no further unit could be added. But if the world continues, further units are added. Ergo, etc. He uses several examples, among them planetary movements and human souls.

If Thomas is right, Bonaventure is not going to be able to prove that it is impossible that the world should always have existed. Nonetheless, again, the two men are in agreement that whatever is opposed to faith is de facto false. The further question whether or no it is also impossible is just that, a further question.

In the *Summa contra gentiles,* Thomas speaks of two kinds of truth about God. One that is derived from what everybody knows, another that is accepted as true because God reveals it. This suggests two distinct, non-overlapping sets of truths. However, if we ask Thomas for examples of naturally knowable truths about God, he will mention "God exists", "There is only one God" etc. Examples of the second kind of truth about God are likely to be the Trinity and the Incarnation. But it is obvious that we cannot maintain this non-overlap.

This leads Thomas to ask two questions: (a) Why did God reveal to us truths about Himself that we could have come to know, truths which even pagan philosophers came to know? (b) Is it reasonable to accept as true things which we cannot know to be true?

The answer to the first question can be surmised if we think of other truths which God has revealed but which are, unlike the truth that God exists, all but self-evident. I have in mind the decalogue. Most of the commandments are, for Thomas, principles of natural law. That means, that they are either self-evidently true or very close to being so-- that is, very easily demonstrable. Well, it is easy for us to see that the sanction of revelation for the great truths of the moral order, even though they are in principle knowable without such help, is all but practically necessary for mankind. Because of sin. Well, sin affects the theoretical reason as well, quite apart from the difficulties of doing metaphysics. Furthermore, even with luck and talent, our chances of getting to the term of philosophy, to natural theology, are slight. But the truth that there is a God is one we need early, middle and late in our lives. Thus, mercifully, God reveals even knowable truths.

The second question provides Thomas with the real significance of the notion that Revelation contains both Preambles and Mysteries. If some of the things God has revealed can be known to be true, it is reasonable to accept the rest, the Mysteries, as true. Here is a proof of the reasonableness of faith.

That proof of the reasonableness of accepting as true things which one does not understand but which God has revealed is reminiscent, as we shall see, of an argument on behalf of Christianity that Pascal devised. But before turning to that, an important precision must be made with respect to St. Thomas Aquinas's attitude toward the God of the philosophers.

Thus far, what we have seen is that (a) he proceeds in the serene confidence that nothing known can conflict with what is believed by the Christian; (b) that if there is a conflict, that is an immediate sign that the knowledge claim is unfounded; (c) but we want to make sure the philosopher is indeed saying something in conflict with the faith. The remarkable fact (d) is that the human mind can, unaided by faith, come to knowledge of God; this is clear from the fact that pagan philosophers have done so. The comparison of natural and supernatural theology is made on the basis of known or believed starting points, but Thomas argues that the contrast is not between what is known and what is revealed because some knowable things have been revealed. Thus, we must distinguish within Revelation the Preambles from the Mysteries.

Now, all of this stresses the great influence Aristotle had on the thought of Aquinas. What of Plato? As we know, that question cannot be answered simply by observing that Thomas had available to him no more Plato than had the men of the previous several centuries. It is true that Plato was not translated and transmitted to the Christian West with the speed and zest that Aristotle was. Bonaventure had a way of commending Plato over Aristotle, saying that while the former was a metaphysician, the latter was merely a philosopher of nature, but we have no reason for thinking Bonaventure would have devoted any more time to the text of Plato, had it been available to him, than he did to that of Aristotle which was at hand. The Plato that functions for Bonaventure is the Plato of the Latin tradition, stemming as much as anything from question 46 of the *83 Diverse Questions* of St. Augustine. The Platonic Ideas become the creative ideas of God and ultimately are one with the Second Person of the Trinity.

The Aristotle of the Treatises is, as you know, occasionally harsh with his long time mentor Plato. He regards the doctrine of Ideas as a category mistake, based on faulty assumptions. At least one motivation for the Ideas, the fact and behavior of shared or common names, can be handled with logical dispatch, a theory of universals being devised that does not seek their counterpart, as universals, outside the human mind. The concept of participation, the essential link between the really real and the evanescent things of this world, is dismissed by Aristotle as an empty metaphor. Does it follow that Thomas Aquinas, who takes Aristotle as his philosophical master, adopts as well these dismissive attitudes toward Platonism?

The answer is no. In recent years, a number of scholars have drawn our attention to the presence within Thomism of a plethora of items of Platonic origin. The notion of participation *pervades* the thought of Thomas. How can this be?

One possible explanation is that Thomism is just an eclectic mess of ideas stemming from different and conflicting traditions, not the much touted synthesis we have heard so much about. Another possibility, urged by some, is that Thomas despite initial appearances is fundamentally a Platonist. My own view, which neatly coincides with the way things are, is that Thomas is fundamentally an Aristotleian and that he takes on Platonism to the extent that it is compatible with that Aristotelianism. I give you two citations. First, the commentary on the *Liber de Causis*, a work Thomas showed is made up of snatches from Proclus *Elements of Theology*. A more Neoplatonic work can scarcely be imagined. Thomas comments on it with care and sympathy. But I invite you to consult the *index nominum* in the Saffrey edition and check out all those references to Aristotle.

Secondly, I refer you to Thomas's proemium to the commentary he wrote on the *De divinis nominibus* of Pseudo-Dionysius. Here we find what might be called Thomas's policy statement on Platonism. Commenting on the obscurity of Denis's style, Thomas says this is not due to incompetence but rather to design: to protect sacred things from the derision of the infidel. Nonetheless, the style and manner of speaking of the text causes difficulty because they are Platonist and uncustomary nowadays. He then gives a brief statement of the Doctrine of Ideas taken as an answer to the Problem of Universals. Then this:

> Haec igitur Platonicorum ratio fidei non consonat nec veritati, quantum ad hoc quod continet de speciebus naturalibus separatis, sed quantum ad id quod dicebant de primo rerum Principio, verissima est eorum opinio et fidei Christianae consona. [This argument of the Platonists agrees neither with faith nor with the truth which respect to what it says of separate natural species,

but with respect to what they said of the First Principle
of things, their opinion is most true and in agreement
with Christian faith.]

In short, Platonism as construed by Augustine is all
right with Thomas. But it is more than that. Platonism
provides Thomas with a great many of the conceptual
tools he needs to say the things that must be said about
our talk of God. A glance at Quaestio 13 of the *Prima
Pars* of the *Summa theologiae* will indicate what I mean.

II

We have now a way in which we must say that, for St.
Thomas Aquinas, there is identity of reference, so to say,
between the God of the philosophers and the God of
Abraham and Isaac. The descriptive phrases which are
employed in sound and successful proofs of God's
existence refer to the God of Jewish and Christian belief.
The God of belief may be described in ways different
from and undreamt of by philosophers -- as e.g. God
incarnate, God triune -- but for Thomas there is even
sometimes identity of descriptive phrase as between
philosophical theology and Revelation. So it looks as if
Thomas is wholly out of sympathy with the point of
Pascal's distinction.

But is that really so? And, even if it were so, is it not
the case that we respond with sympathy to Pascal's
statement? Sometimes the sympathy can lend to a
standpoint which is clearly incompatible with the views
of Thomas Aquinas. Often, what people hear in Pascal,
is the echo of what they take to be the evident fact that
the existence of God cannot be proved. "Of course you
can't prove that God exists." How often I have heard
that confident remark over the years. Coming from a

Catholic, it is to say the least surprising -- though not necessarily culpable or even blameworthy, given the parlous state of religious education in recent years. Nonetheless, it should be no secret that, for the Roman Catholic, it is *de fide* that human beings can from their knowledge of what has been made come to knowledge of the invisible things of God. Paul (Rom.ans, I:20) was used, as we saw earlier, by the Fathers of Vatican I to make that point. That is why it is not a matter of opinion, but of faith, that God can come to be known from knowledge of the world without the aid of Revelation.

I mentioned earlier that Pascal fashions an argument on behalf of Christianity that is reminiscent of Thomas's argument that it is reasonable to accept as true on God's authority what we do not understand. I refer to course to the famous *pari de Pascal.* Pascal rightly holds that no direct proof of the truth of Christianity can be had, as if it could be seen as true independently of faith. Nonetheless, Pascal says, we can see that it would be irrational not to accept it as true. Christianity includes essentially talk of an eternal reward which comes to those who accept it. All right. If you accept it as true and it turns out to be true, you win eternally. If you accept is as true and it turns out to be false, you are not there to lose. If however you reject it as false and it turns out to be true, you lose forever. The only rational thing to do, therefore, is to accept Christianity as true.

I hasten to add that I don't think Pascal was any more impressed by this than you are. Accepting Christianity as true is not like buying a ticket in the Lottery. Faith relates us to a personal God, as our creator and savior. When we think of someone coming to be a Christian, we do not imagine them grudgingly conceding that some argument is valid and sound. We speak of conversion, not of changing our mind.

There, I think, is the source of Pascal's appeal. It has nothing to do with whether or not there are sound proofs for the existence of God. There have been men -- Cardinal Newman and C.S. Lewis among them -- who held that there are sound proofs for God's existence but who also say that such proofs played no role in their conversion. Of course they didn't. Not immediately. How could they? Speculative truths are not proximate principles of action. The analogy we need is found in the moral order.

It is a sad fact of everyone's experience, that knowing what we ought to do and doing it are not the same thing. We may see or come to see that a certain kind of behavior is inappropriate for a rational agent. Let us say we change our minds about such behavior. The moral task is more onerous. We must change our lives. No argument can do that for us. We change our moral character not in the quince it takes to see that an argument is sound, but only gradually, as the result of repeated acts of the same kind. The only way to learn how to play the harp is to play the harp. The Romantic thinks that he can be a hero by enacting in fantasy heroic acts. We may emerge from theaters with the uptilted chin of one who has done great things. But heroism is not achieved in imagination. Kierkegaard distinguished between thought and existence. Existence is the moral order, the order of action. To change our lives is a task very unlike changing our minds -- which can be difficult enough in its own way.

Such considerations enable us to see why Pascal, within the *Pari* passage, goes on to say how it is that one becomes a Christian. Say your prayers, he urges, use Holy Water, attend Mass. It is as if he were saying: in order to become a Christian perform the acts of a Christian. This is not Pelagianism. Grace would no doubt already be operative in one's ability to perform one such act.

What I am suggesting, then, is that we respond as we do to Pascal because we know the vast difference there is between conversion, moral or religious, and the theoretical use of our mind, fashioning sound arguments, etc. It does not follow that there are not sound proofs of God's existence. It certainly does not follow that the realm of faith is wholly distinct from and utterly indifferent to the realm of reason. That would be, or would soon lead to, the fideism the Church has always condemned.

FIVE

THE DEGREES OF PRACTICAL KNOWLEDGE

Les degres du savoir puts before the mind of its reader a vast panorama of spiritual activity, of modes of wisdom, ranging from the natural sciences through metaphysics to the contemplation of the mystic. If these various degrees of wisdom are distinguished, however, we are asked not to be content with their otherness, but to see beyond to the way in which they hang together and cohere. The actual title of Maritain's masterpiece is *Distinguer pour unir ou les degres du savoir*, which I cite from the 8th revised and augmented edition, Paris, 1963.

I want to say a few things about Maritain's moral epistemology as it is conveyed by *Les degres du savoir*. As it happens, it is in the course of his discussion of mysticism that Maritain says the things which form the basis of my remarks. Maritain contrasts St. Thomas Aquinas and St. John of the Cross by calling the former the Master of Communicable Wisdom and the latter the Master of Incommunicable Wisdom. In explaining what he means by these epithets, Maritain introduces the topic of the speculative and the practical. (p. 616) The text is concerned with this distinction in a formal way for only a few pages (pp. 618-627), but those pages are supplemented by *Annexe VII*, which is considerably more extensive (pp. 901-918). If the whole work is concerned with degrees of wisdom, these remarks may be said to deal with the degrees of practical knowledge. What I propose to do is (1) convey as swiftly and accurately as I can the content of the two passages just mentioned; (2) say a few things about the relation of Maritain's doctrine to its sources in the writings of Thomas Aquinas; and (3) suggest the way the whole moral order is unified by Maritain's employment of the concept of degrees of practical knowledge.

No student of these passages in *Les degres du savoir* can afford to overlook the remarkable work of Yves Simon, *La critique de la connaissance morale*. It had been my intention to develop my paper as a detailed comparison of the doctrine of Maritain and its interpretation and development by Simon. There are not a few occasions when the explanation of the disciple is clearer than the teaching of the master. I am reminded of the anecdote according to which Charlie Chaplin entered a Charlie Chaplin look-alike contest -- and came in third. It takes nothing from either Maritain or Simon to notice that while the former is often inchoative, suggestive, intuitive, the latter excels in clarity, prolongation and rational precision. Although my paper does not develop along the lines of such a comparison of the two men, my high estimate of Simon's discussion of Maritain's doctrine leads me to make this special mention of it. I

cannot believe that my own understanding of Maritain
is unaffected by a quarter of a century of admiration for
La critique de la connaissance morale.

I

In the speculative order, the mind, taking its rise from
the existent world, causes to lift up from this world
universes of intelligibility more and more pure, with
purity read in terms of distance from matter. Maritain
has in mind the distinction of speculative science into
natural philosophy, mathematics and metaphysics. The
degrees of speculative knowledge, accordingly, are
spoken of in terms of degrees of abstraction from matter.
The movement in the practical order, on the other hand,
is toward concrete existence, toward human acts
accomplished in the world of particularity from which
speculative thinking progressively distances itself. In
the practical order, it is not simply knowledge that is
wanted, but a knowledge ordered to the direction or
guidance of human action.

Maritain distinguishes three levels of practical
knowing: practical philosophy or moral philosophy,
which he characterizes as *speculatively practical*; what he
calls *practically practical* science, and finally *prudence.*
"The virtue of prudence is right practical knowledge as
immediately regulative of action." (p. 623) Actually,
Maritain first establishes a distinction between
speculatively practical science and prudence. If both are
action guiding, speculatively practical science is so only
remotely, from afar, whereas, as we have just seen,
prudence is the immediate guide of the concrete act *hic
et nunc.* (p. 621) The question then arises whether there
is a science, a practical science, between speculatively
practical science and prudence. The notion of *practically*

practical science expresses Maritain's affirmative answer to this question, an answer prompted by St. Thomas Aquinas. "...it's no longer a matter of explaining, of resolving even a practical truth into its causes and principles. It's a matter of preparing action and assigning its proximate rules." (p. 624)

Now, speculatively practical science is a type common to the three moral sciences recognized by Aristotle: ethics, economics, and politics. What then would be examples of practically practical sciences? Maritain first lists some authors: Montaigne, Pascal, Nietzsche, Shakespeare, Racine, Baudelaire, Swift, Meredith, Balzac, Dostoevsky. These men should not be thought of as disinterested observers or psychologists but as moralists, not in the sense of moral philosophers but rather in the sense of practioners (*practiciens*) of the science of morals. "For it is the very dynamism of the human being that they study, the use of free will itself, and therefore man's relation to his ends such that the exactitude and depth of their views depend not only on the acuity of their gaze but on their ideas of good and evil and on the dispositions of their own hearts with regard to the sovereign good." (p. 627) It is clear how the concept of practically practical science will serve Maritain in his characterization of the writings of St. John of the Cross by contrast with those of St. Thomas.

"Because practical knowledge is like a continuous movement of thought which descends toward concrete action in order to make it exist, its practical character, present from its origin, gradually intensifies until in *prudence* it becomes totally dominant." (p. 901) This is how *Annexe VII* begins and far more clearly than in the text the practical order is seen as, so to say, the reverse of the speculative. If the speculative moves away from the concrete and the material, up through philosophy of nature and mathematics to metaphysics, the practical is the movement toward the ever more concrete which reaches its term in prudence, the immediate guide of action. A new note is struck now; what completes the practicality of the practical is the will. Practical knowledge at all levels is action guiding, but it guides action more and more proximately as we move toward the realm of prudence.

Moral philosophy is speculatively practical knowledge as opposed to practically practical knowledge which includes practically practical moral sciences as well as prudence, the prime instance of the practically practical. Moral philosophy remains intellectual in the sense that its truth does not imply nor engage right appetite nor affective motion. If practical truth consists in the judgment's conformity with rectified appetite, then moral philosophy is not truth with practical truth. Maritain speaks of moral philosophy as scrutinizing its objects according to the laws of ontological analysis, *dividendo et resolvendo*, that is scrutinizing them in a speculative manner. The following passage lays out the degrees of practical knowing as Maritain sees them.

> If truth in practical philosophy does not consists purely and simply in *cognoscere* as it does in speculative philosophy, it at least consists in *cognoscere* as the foundation of *dirigere*, whereas in practically practical knowledge it already consists in *dirigere* but precisely as founded in *cognoscere*, and in prudence it formally consists in the *dirigere* itself. (p. 905)

Maritain takes this to mean that the operable thing can be considered, as operable, in three ways. Finally, he repeats that the phrase "practically practical" applies in a loose sense to those moralists and novelists listed earlier but in the strict sense only to prudence. There is, accordingly, a gradual sharpening of the terminology or, as in this case, making it more supple. Maritain began by asking of there was an intermediary between practical science and prudence. The answer was yes and the suggestion was that we call the intermediary knowledge practically practical. Now we learn that, in the strict sense, it is prudence that is practically practical.

It is no easy matter to grasp what precisely it is that Maritain means by the practically practical as opposed to the speculatively practical and to prudence. Sometimes he illustrates what he means by distinguishing between theoretical and practical medicine. The former would define and order and schematize such things as fevers whereas the latter would prescribe such and such a potion to relieve a fever or perhaps remove the cause of the fever.

The analogue of this in morals would be theoretical ethics and practical ethics. Presumably, theoretical ethics would be characterized not simply by its greater remoteness from the action it would direct, its greater generality, but also by the fact that it proceeds *dividendo et definiendo*. But Maritain explicitly rejects this interpretation. "...when St. Thomas speaks of the *speculative manner* of considering an object of operation, he isn't thinking of the knowledge we are calling here speculatively practical, for example moral philosophy...he is thinking if a *purely speculative* knowledge of an object which nonetheless is operable." (p. 909) The mode of both speculatively practical and practically practical science is compositive as opposed to resolutive.

Maritain exemplifies the distinction by appealing to the difference between the moral theology of Thomas Aquinas in the Second Part of the *Summa theologiae* and the moral theology of ian Alphonsus Ligouri. One senses what it is that the distinction is meant to pick out. Surely the procedure of both the *Prima secundae* and the *Secunda secundae* is sufficiently different from that of a man giving quite circumstantial and concrete advice. Is the difference one of degree or one of kind? Maritain phrases the question in this way: Is the *habitus* of moral philosophy identical to the *habitus* of practically practical moral science. He holds that it is probable that these are different *habitus* (and that prudence is a third *habitus* distinct from them both). Somewhat surprisingly, perhaps, given the origin of the distinction, he feels sure that there is no such distinction of habitus between practically practical science in the realm of the *factibile* or art. This distinction between the *agibile* and *factibile*, between the practically practical and completely practical in the two realms, is yet more surprising when we consider that earlier (pp. 906-7), the distinction between practically practical and completely practical had been attached to the distinction between *facultas* and *usus*. But then Maritain had been quick to add, "Except insofar as it concerns prudence which is different from art in that it extends to actual exercise, since not to use prudence *hic et nunc* would be imprudence." (p. 907, n. 1)

The distinction between the speculatively practical and the practically practical is sometimes put like this: while the speculatively practical is completely intellectual, the practically practical already involves the appetitive condition of the knower, though not in the complete way that prudence does. "The rectitude of willing is doubtless *more* required by prudence, which alone considers the singular case *hic et nunc* and which alone descends to the *imperium*. But it is also necessary, for reasons just given, for practically practical science." (p. 915, n. 1) Nonetheless, Maritain allows that sometimes the practioners of practically practical science give bad advice and are wrong to a greater or lesser degree. This of course is incompatible with the claim that such sciences depend upon the rectitude of the will.

There are, then, difficulties with the threefold distinction Maritain wishes to make in the practical order. The distinction between moral philosophy and prudence poses no problem. It is the nature and status of practically practical science that puzzles Maritain's reader. This is not to say that he cannot easily see what it is Maritain wishes the phrase to denote. When we consider, for example, the distinction Thomas Aquinas made between the judgment *per modum cognitionis* and the judgment *per modum connaturalitatis* in the matter of chastity, we seem to be confronted with two sorts of advice, that of the moral theologian and that of the chaste man. The chaste man in the case in point is not judging concerning some action of his own. Rather he is putting himself into the shoes of his questioner and, guided by his own rectified appetite, giving a judgment as to what is to be done. What is to be done by another, that is, not *hic et nunc* by himself. No need to mention the use Maritain put connaturality to in many areas beyond that in which it functions for St. Thomas Aquinas. Surely, when connaturality is used to distinguish between the judgment of prudence and advice given by the good man which is in effect some version of, "Well, what I would do is..." we encounter little or no difficulty in recognizing a type of moral knowledge which falls between moral philosophy and the judgment of prudence as such. The question is not whether there is such intermediate knowledge but how best to characterize it. Let us turn now to the texts of St. Thomas which inspired Maritain and see if they cast light on his notion of practically practical knowledge.

II

The second part of *Annexe VII* begins with a list of texts on which Maritain relies for his understanding of the distinction between the speculative and practical as well as for his views on the degrees of practical knowledge. We find (on p. 907) a schema devised to show the distinction between speculative and practical knowledge and to lay out for us the degrees of practical knowledge. What is the relation between Maritain's view that practical knowledge is of three kinds or degrees and the distinction to be found in the text cited from *Summa theologiae,* Ia, q. 14, a. 16? Thomas, asking whether God has speculative or practical knowledge of creatures, begins by making the distinction that interests us.

> Knowledge can be called speculative *first* because of the things known, which are not operable by the knower, as is the case with man's knowledge of natural or divine things. *Second,* because of the way of knowing, as for example if a builder should think of a house by defining and distinguishing, considering its universal characteristics. This is to consider operable objects in a speculative way and not insofar as they are operable. For something is operable thanks to an application of form to matter, not by analyzing a composite thing into its universal formal principles.

Maritain stops quoting at this point, but the text itself goes on as follows:

> *Third,* with respect to the end. For the practical intellect differs from the speculative in its end, as has been said. The practical intellect is ordered to the end of the operation whereas the end of the speculative intellect is the consideration of truth. Thus if a builder were to consider how a house can come into being, not committing himself to operation as his end but to knowledge alone, his consideration would be, from the point of view of its end, speculative, though bearing on an operable object.

Clearly, since there is a plurality of criteria for speculative and practical knowledge, there is the possibility of there being degrees of both. That is, a given instance of knowing can be, with regard to one or more criteria, speculative and with regard to others practical, and vice versa. Of course, a given instance of knowing can be speculative or practical with regard to all criteria and thus be either completely speculative or completely practical. This text of St. Thomas seems just what we need if we want a way of speaking of degrees of practical knowing.

We can also see why Maritain did not quote the second portion of text, which goes on to discuss the end as a criterion: Maritain had already discussed the end before setting down his schema. Maritain is influenced by a remark of Cajetan's in the cardinal's commentary on the passage before us. Cajetan distinguishes between the *finis cognitionis vel scientiae* and the *finis cognoscentis vel scientis,* between the end of the knowledge and the end of the knower. Maritain accepts the importance of this distinction and argues that it is only the ordination of knowledge to an end other than knowledge that epistemology or noetics has to consider. Whether or not an agent actually uses this knowledge to achieve the end toward which the knowledge is ordered is a matter of free will and cannot enter into the specification of a *habitus.* (p. 906-7. In a footnote on p. 907, Maritain observes that this distinction does not seem applicable to prudence.) It may be that Maritain is misled by Cajetan here and tends to conflate two of the criteria set down by St. Thomas, namely, manner of consideration and end, since the manner of considering provides the ordination to operation Cajetan seems to mean by the *finis scientiae.*

What on the basis of the text of St. Thomas might one give as the degrees of practical knowledge? The object considered is either something we can do or make, or it is not. If it is, it is an operable object and knowledge of it will be so far practical. But the way of knowing the operable object may be either by way of dividing and defining and classifying or in an action guiding manner, e.g. a knowledge expressed in precepts. The latter would be instances of what Thomas means by a compositive way of knowing. Thus to know an operable object in a compositive manner is to know it more practically than to know it in a resolutive or analytical manner. Thirdly, if one is actually putting this knowledge to use, is acting on it, then his end or purpose is practical. Knowledge can only be put to use if it is knowledge of an operable object in a compositive manner, so we are faced here with completely practical knowledge.

How does this stratification of practical knowledge compare with Maritain's? Let us call the degrees of practical knowing suggested by the text of St. Thomas *minimally practical knowledge, virtually practical knowledge* and *completely practical knowledge*. Is minimally practical knowledge identical with Maritain's speculatively practical knowledge? Perhaps; then again, perhaps not. On the one hand, Maritain explicitly denies that moral philosophy which is an instance of speculatively practical knowledge can be characterized as knowing an operable object in a speculative way. But to define virtue, to discuss the species of a given virtue, are instances of minimally practical knowledge and are clearly activities we associate with moral philosophy. Need we take Maritain's denial literally? If not, it is fairly clear that minimally practical and speculatively practical knowledge can be identified.

Equally, I think, we can identify what in both divisions is called completely practical knowledge -- at least when we are talking of moral knowledge.

Completely practical knowledge in the moral order will be manifested by prudence -- or its opposite.

So we come back to practically practical knowledge. Is it identical with virtually practical knowledge? The difficulty with saying it is stems from Maritain's wish to have practically practical knowledge be manifested in advice of a concrete and particular nature, though at some low level of generality. But "Good is to be done and pursued and evil avoided," the first and most general principle of the practical order, seems to satisfy the criteria of virtually practical knowledge. It is action guiding advice although of a breathtaking order of generality. Indeed, if we consider the famous text in *Summa theologiae*, IaIIae, q. 94, a. 2, which asks whether there is one or many precepts of natural law, we will note a progression from the *ratio boni* (the good is that which all things desire) to the first precept (good is to be done and evil avoided). Definitions, divisions, classifications. are presupposed to the formulation of practical precepts. If precepts save the two criteria of virtually practical knowing -- operable object and compositive mode -- there would seem to be homogeneity in practical knowing from the most to the least general sort of advice. This suggests that what we have called minimally practical knowledge should be regarded as a moment in moral philosophy, not as a rival to it. Moral philosophy is best seen as aiming to give very general advice, at the outset, and continues toward the concrete by giving more and more circumstantial advice as to what should be done and what avoided. On the basis of the text of St. Thomas, there is no way one could distinguish between what Maritain calls speculatively practical and practically practical knowledge. Both would be concerned with an operable object in a compositive way; the fact that one is more general than the other does not seem to provide a basis for formally distinguishing the two.

III

Maritain came up with his schema of degrees of practical knowledge, not precisely as exegesis of St. Thomas, but as inspired by Thomas. I can find no claim in the passages of *Les degres du savoir* I am examining to the effect that Maritain intends to give an accurate restatement of the views of St. Thomas. That his schema is not identical with the one we can construct from Thomas is sufficiently clear. Thus, it is not on an exegetical level that we will find the value and power of what Maritain has to say.

What especially lends his position weight is his insistence that, however we distinguish degrees or types or levels of practical knowing, we are dealing with something unified, something which coheres. Maritain is far more interested, finally, in that concrete coherence than he is in abstract distinctions. This is evident, I think, in the offhand but recurrent remark found both in the text and in the *Annexe* to the effect that Maritain does not think that any purely philosophical ethics can address itself to man's actual condition. I want to draw my considerations to a close by showing that, whatever difficulties we find in relating his various remarks to one another, Maritain's conception of practically practical science draws our attention to a fact about moral science it would be very difficult to ignore.

One of the points of the doctrine of natural law is to show that men, despite their fallen moral condition whether taken singly or as a society, can arrive at some true knowledge as to what is fulfilling of the kind of agent we are. Bad morals are unable to completely snuff out a person's capacity to form true judgments as to what he ought to do. But such judgments are very general, so general that they do not engage, or threaten, our moral character. The womanizer can when jaded wax eloquent on the attractions of chastity. More particular judgments, however, can have applications to the judge he will find difficult to ignore, and the more difficult as the judgments become more circumstantial. Indeed, if our moral character is bad, we may be incapable of formulating particular practical judgments appropriate to our own condition. In the case of particular judgments bearing on the singular, this is easy to see. *Qualis unusquisque est, talis finis ei videtur.* Our singular judgments manifest our moral character. Only the good man can truly perceive the demands of the good in concrete singular circumstances.

What Maritain's conception of practically practical science draws attention to is a further fact. Even at the level of theory and generalization what we say will by and large reflect what we are. What is called rationalization is only one instance of this, but it is a sufficient instance. Are we not often aware that we are tailoring our *general* conceptions of what is to be done or avoided to what our acquired dispositions demand? If this is so, it will be all the more so in the example St. Thomas gives of a man giving advice on the demands of chastity, not *per modum cognitionis* but *per modum inclinationis*. His advice will reflect what he is, not just what he knows. One of the lessons of Maritain's conception of the practically practical, as applied to moral knowledge, is that our judgments *per modum cognitionis* may also, in their own way, reflect what we are.

S I X

THE PRIMACY OF THE COMMON GOOD

The title of this chapter is meant to recall a famous controversy of some forty years ago that involved Jacques Maritain, Yves Simon, I. Thomas Eschmann, O.P. and Charles DeKoninck. Three of these men were connected with the University of Notre Dame. Jacques Maritain regularly lectured here and in 1957 was present at the inauguration of the Jacques Maritain Center. Yves Simon was a professor in the philosophy department before going to the University of Chicago -- though he never left South Bend -- and Charles DeKoninck in the late 50's and early 60's divided his academic year between Laval University in Quebec and Notre Dame. I shall approach the doctrine of the common good by way of a review of some aspects of the controversy involving these men.

They were all Thomists. That is, having taken note of the Church's naming of St. Thomas Aquinas as, in a special way, the guide and patron of Catholic intellectual life, they devoted themselves to the study of his work, not as historians, not as antiquarians, but as seekers after truths that travel, truths that while encountered in a medieval setting could, with appropriate and linguistic adjustments, be made to speak to modern man and his problems.

Maritain once wrote," *Vae mihi si non thomistizavero.*" ["Woe is me if I should cease to be a Thomist"] and DeKoninck wrote, "I hope so to understand Saint Thomas as to remain always a disciple who trusts his master." Well, the French express themselves in dramatic ways, and the Flemish too, but let no one imagine that these statement express a policy of intellectual servitude or dogmatism. Neither man held any position *because* St. Thomas held it.

I mention this to suggest the ambience in which the best Catholic intellectual work has been done. Within a tradition, certainly, but interpreting, expanding and developing that tradition. "Tradition and the Individual Talent," T.S. Eliot's essay dealing with the way in which a poet both belongs to and alters the tradition in which he writes, makes a point both Maritain and DeKoninck would accept wholeheartedly. That a sympathetic reading of common sources does not produce identical understandings is clear from the dispute that arose over Maritain's effort to develop a Catholic, even Thomistic, personalism.

The most pertinent books by Maritain are *Three Reformers,* published in Paris in 1925; *Du regime temporel et la liberte,* Paris, 1933; *Humanisme Integral,* Paris, 1936; *Scholasticism and Politics,* New York, 1939; *Les droits de l'homme et la loi naturelle,* Paris, 1947; *La personne et le bien commun,* Paris, 1947.

Individual and Person

Maritain's efforts to develop a personalism were intended to provide an alternative to what he did not shrink from calling the divinization of the individual in modern thought and practice which had led to a divinization of the state. In "La conquete de la liberte," [*Principes d'une politique humaniste*, New York, 1944.] Maritain wrote of the false political emancipation and false conception of human rights which derive from the anthropocentrism of Rousseau and Kant based on the autonomy of the human person. One is free if he obeys only himself. Maritain cited three political and social consequences of this divinization of the individual: (1) a practical atheism in society, since God appears as a threat to the autonomy of the individual; (2) the theoretical and practical disappearance of the idea of the common good; (3) the theoretical and practical disappearance of the idea of authority. The notion of the Mass Man and of a leader who is an inhuman monster follow. Bourgeois liberalism thus paves the way for revolutionary totalitarianism.

This is stern stuff. Maritain is asserting that the political horrors of this century are a consequence of a false understanding of person and society and that they can only be effectively combated with a true understanding. Here is Maritain's summary statement of that true alternative.

> True political emancipation, on the contrary, or the true city of human rights, takes for its principle a conception of the autonomy of the person in conformity with the nature of things and thus theocentric. Given this, obedience in the service of justice is not opposed to liberty, but is rather the normal way to achieve it. Man must progressively achieve a liberty which in the social

and political order chiefly consists in his becoming as independent as given historical conditions permit of the constraints of material nature. In short, the human person inasmuch as he is made for God and to participate in absolute goods, transcends the earthly society of which he is a member, yet insofar as he is what he is thanks to that society, he is *part* of society as of a larger and better whole. [*ibid.*, p. 30]

A theocentric view, one that sees man as part of society but also as ordered to absolute goods, provides a sounder conception of man as citizen of the earthly and heavenly cities. The essay from which I quote was published in 1944, but the thoughts expressed were already familiar ones in Maritain's writings. In *Scholasticism and Politics*, citing a distinction between *individuality* and *personality*, Maritain insists that the "*humanism of the individual* and *democracy of the individual* in which the twentieth century had placed its hopes, must be replaced today -- if we want to save civilization -- by *humanism of the person* and *democracy of the person*." [*Scholasticism and Politics*, p. 56] That distinction between individual and person is already present in the essay on Luther in *Three Reformers* in 1925 and in *Du regime temporel et liberte* in 1933, in *Humanisme Integral* in 1936, as well as in *Les droits de l'homme et la loi naturelle* in 1942. But , if it was already a distinction prominent in his writings, it was now put to a crucial use.

Any student of Jacques Maritain's writings will know that ideas that appear early in his thought and continue to be used throughout his long career often undergo development over time, becoming clearer and more subtle. But sometimes in later writings Maritain will simply take over whole passages from earlier works, indicating satisfaction with the earlier statement. Sometimes, however, an idea will wax and wane as far as clarity goes and then it seems a good principle of interpretation to let passages comment on one another without exclusive regard for chronology. In the case of Maritain's distinction in man between individual and person, which has such a long career in his writings, we have an instance of the third kind. It is not always the later expressions which are the clearest and there are certainly some statements of the contrast which invite criticism.

The contrast between individual and person is used for a variety of purposes, but an abiding note is that it will help us avoid an anthropocentric humanism or personalism, one that is effectively atheist, and to embrace in its stead a theocentric humanism or personalism. The social and political consequence of the contrast is that man is a part of civil society as individual, but as person transcends that common good.

Furthermore, man as individual relates to material goods, but as person he relates to spiritual goods. Pascal said "the ego is hateful" whereas Thomas held that the person is that which is noblest in the whole of nature. "It is this material pole, and the *individual* becoming the center of all things, that the words of Pascal aim at. And it is on the contrary with the spiritual pole, and with the *person*, source of freedom and of goodness, that the words of St. Thomas are concerned." [ibid p. 58]

The individuality of things is rooted in matter; matter sets off thing from thing; it is an appetite for what benefits the individual as such. "In so far as we are individuals, each of us is a fragment of a species, a part of this universe, a single dot in the immense network of forces and influences, cosmic, ethnic, historic, whose laws we obey. We are subject to the determinism of the physical world. But each man is also a person and, in so far as he is a person, he is not subject to the stars and the atoms; for he subsists entirely with the very subsistence of his spiritual soul, and the latter is in him a principle of creative unity, of independence and of freedom." [ibid p. 58]

Since Maritain works with the definition of person that had been bequeathed to the Scholastics by Boethius -- *a person is an individual substance of a rational nature*; that is, a person is a kind of individual -- the contrast he wants to draw presents difficulties. It is not simply a matter of distinguishing those individuals who are persons from those who are not -- men from monkeys, say -- but rather two ways of looking at man.

The contrast is not meant to point to two distinct *things* -- man as individual, man as person -- so much as to draw a moral contrast. Man as individual is grasping, acquisitive, egocentric; man as person is open to the spiritual. Maritain quotes with approval this passage from Garrigou-Lagrange: "Man will be fully a person, a *per se subsistens* and a *per se operans*, only in so far as the life of reason and liberty dominates that of the senses and passions in him; otherwise he will remain like the animal, a simple *individual*, the slave of events and circumstances, always led by something else, incapable of guiding himself; he will be only a part, without being able to aspire to the whole." [*Three Reformers*, p. 24] To be an individual thus appears to be a morally defective state for which one is responsible, and to be a person a morally praiseworthy condition.

It is this that renders others passages which make social and political applications hard to understand. "Thus the individual in each of us, taken as an individual member of the city, exists for his city and ought at need to sacrifice his life for it, as for instance in a just war. But taken as a person whose destiny is God, the city exists for him, to wit, for the advancement of the moral and spiritual life and the heaping up of divine goods." [ibid p. 22] Here what pertains to man as individual and what pertains to him as person seem fixed and more or less definitional.

But what is puzzling about Maritain's position is that he seems to hold that man is both subordinate to the common good and that he transcends it. Consider the following from *Three Reformers*.

> On the contrary, according to the principles of St. Thomas, it is because he is first an individual of a species that man, having need of the help of his fellows to perfect his specific activity, is consequently an *individual* of the city, a member of society. And on this count he is subordinated to the good of his city as to the good of the whole, the common good which as such is more *divine* and therefore better deserving the love of each than his very own life. But if it is a question of the destiny which belongs to man as a *person*, the relation is inverse, and it is the human city which is subordinate to his destiny. If every human person is made directly, as to his first and proper good, for God, Who is his ultimate end, and 'the distinct common good' of the entire universe, he ought not therefore, on this count, in accordance with the law of charity, to prefer anything to himself save God. So much so that according as personality is realized in any being, to that extent does it become an independent whole and not a part (whatever be its ties on other grounds). [ibid.]

A puzzling position. Human development seems portrayed as a matter of escaping the net of society and its demands and relating oneself to spiritual goods, preeminently to God, with the result that only God can be preferred to oneself.

The Controversy

The difficulties and complexities of Maritain's contrast of individual and person with its implications for the common good invited criticism. And, in 1943, that criticism came in the form of a small book, Charles DeKoninck's *De la primaute du bien common*, published in Quebec. The nub of the book had already been presented to L'Academie Canadienne Saint-Thomas d'Aquin in October, 1942, as "La notion du bien commun," but the issue of the proceedings in which it appeared was not published until 1945. The 1943 book contained that essay and another, "The Principle of the New Order." The subtitle of DeKoninck's book was significant: Against the Personalists. Was it an attack on Maritain? Maritain is not mentioned either in the original presentation or in the book. Nevertheless, two eminent philosophers took it to be an attack on Maritain and rose to his defense.

Yves Simon, writing in *The Review of Politics* (Vol. VI, 1944, pp. 530-533), had praise for DeKoninck's interpretation, finding that "it constitutes a very sound foundation for any further development of the theory of the common good" and adding that "insofar as DeKoninck's essay vindicates the primacy of the common good and carries out the criticism of definite positions, it is entirely praiseworthy." Indeed, Simon characterizes the target of DeKoninck's attack as "vicious stupidities" and "monstrosities." We are not surprised, accordingly, that Simon does not consider Maritain's views to fall within the target area. Nonetheless, Simon laments the fact that the book's subtitle, "Against the Personalists," could invite the interpretation that Maritain *is* its target, or one of its targets, because Maritain has embraced a kind of personalism. The views attacked by DeKoninck are as odious to Maritain as to anyone else and it would be pure calumny to suggest otherwise.

There is then a possible interpretation of DeKoninck's book that could have been cleared up in a quince. But, alas, the Dominican I. Thomas Eschmann decided to enter the debate with his "In Defense of Jacques Maritain." [*The Modern Schoolman* XXIII, 4, 1945, pp. 183-208.] Father Eschmann maintained that the position DeKoninck attacked was that of Maritain, indeed that of St. Thomas Aquinas and all the Fathers for the past two thousand years, and Eschmann proceeds to defend the position.

Did DeKoninck intend to attack Maritain anonymously, as a personalist? Is the position he attacked accepted or rejected by Maritain? I do not know the answer to the first question for certain, but I am confident the answer is no. DeKoninck meant to attack Personalism. Eschmann's piece could scarcely be ignored, since his claim was that DeKoninck had misunderstood St. Thomas, fighting words to any Thomist, and Dekoninck replied in a lengthy piece, "In Defense of St. Thomas." [*Laval theologique et philosophique*, I,2, pp. 3-103.] The tone is unfortunate, however much it echoes that of Eschmann's; moreover the reply to Eschmann is longer than the original book and is structured by Eschmann's charges. Maritain does not figure in the exposition. It is fair to say that DeKoninck demolished Eschmann. It is also clear that Maritain does not hold the positions Eschmann attributes to him, certainly not in the explicit way the Dominican embraces them. When Maritain wrote *The Person and the Common Good* in 1947 he expressed himself with a great deal of clarity on points that had figured in the controversy. It is therefore puzzling that the only

allusion he makes to the controversy is oblique. In a
footnote, he thanks Father Eschmann for defending him
while insisting that the positions attacked are not his!

> I thank the author of these lines for having defended
> me in a lively debate which took place in Canada and the
> United States. It was curiously the case that in
> criticizing ideas which are not mine, it was obliquely
> suggested they were even though my name was not
> mentioned. I hope that the present essay, by correcting
> some excessive formulations I myself never used, will put
> an end to misunderstandings and confusions indigenous
> to such controversies.

This is an extremely Delphic remark. Maritain thanks
Eschmann, who ascribed to Maritain the positions
DeKoninck attacked, but which Maritain never held,
and hopes in the present work to correct excessive
formulations he never used (and which presumably
Eschmann had). Without naming DeKoninck, Maritain
suggests that DeKoninck was attacking him, though
DeKoninck did not name Maritain nor attribute the
positions he criticized to Maritain either in the original
book or in the reply to Eschmann. The temperature of
this controversy was raised by Eschmann's rhetoric
which prevented any fruitful exchange. Simon's review
is straightforward and civil and one can imagine a
wholly different sequel if Eschmann had not muddied
the waters.

In a letter he wrote to Maritain on December 11, 1945,
Yves Simon relates a conversation he had with Jacques
de Monleon in Quebec the previous summer. In it
Simon summed up the doctrine on the common good in
five propositions on which "there is complete agreement
between you, me, Dekoninck and himself." The five
points are: (1) Any good of a higher order is greater
than any good of a lower order. (2) Within a given

order, there is absolute primacy of the common good over any private good. (3) When a person is an absolute person (God), there is an absolute coincidence of common and personal good. (4) To the degree that a created person is a person there is a tendency toward a coincidence of personal and common good. (5) There is no restriction on the primacy of the common good in its order; when the primacy disappears (as in 3 and 4), this is not because the primacy then belongs to a private good, but that the problem of primacy disappears. Simon was convinced from first to last that there was this fundamental agreement and that any suggestion that there was not was libelous. There is little doubt that Simon agreed with the major contentions of DeKoninck's book and was certain Maritain himself did. Why then did Maritain extend thanks to Eschmann and not to Yves Simon? Surely Simon was in the right and Eschmann in the wrong.

Person and Common Good

Beyond the five points of difference of expression, this controversy conveys the centrality of the common good, indeed, the primacy of the common good. What these Thomists are as one in opposing is the liberated individual of modern thought, the Kantian person who has become his own end, the autonomous individual presupposed by contract theory, the Marxist person for whom all claims other than private ones are alienations to be overcome -- God and society and family deprive me of what is proper to me and they must be overcome.

Such a view of the human person, of the individual of a rational nature, tends to look at societal relations, politics and political economy, as devices whereby the

good of the individual as such can be most prudently
achieved. The social contract is something I enter into
for my own good, my own proper good. The notion of
the common good is thereby denatured and becomes a
mere abstraction. By that I mean that it becomes some
such claim as this: It is common to all individuals to look
out for Number One.

In our tradition, on the contrary, man is by nature a
political animal. He is a part of a larger whole, not by
choice, but of necessity -- he could not otherwise come
into existence and survive. Human persons do not fall
out of the sky to confront one another and the
possibility of a social contract. They are born to mothers,
nurtured at the breast, raised and educated by father
and mother, brought from total dependency to the point
where they can be responsible members of the social
groups to which they belong.   Moral autonomy,
according to this view, is not a matter of progressively
weakening links to others, but of developing them in
terms of what is truly perfective and fulfilling of the
kind of entity a human person is.

Even this beginning of a sketch makes it clear why the
Church is opposed both to *laissez-faire* capitalism and to
socialism. Both are grounded on a defective notion of
the person and therefore of society.   An economic
system that aimed at profit only and saw others merely
as objects of exploitation on the way to amassing more
and more wealth without end would put the private
good of the pursuer of wealth not only above the private
goods of all others but also above the goods shared by
many. But of course such would deny that there is any
good perfective of members of society which is not
simply the private good of any of them, goods like peace
and order. One who wants peace and order simply as a
means to self-aggrandizement does not want them as
common goods.

Classical socialism sees persons as mere units, without history, without family, without any features independent of their being parts of the invented social whole.   Any discrimination between persons on the basis of property or talent or gender becomes abhorrent. It is Mass Man who becomes the ideal -- the featureless constituent of the social machine.

It will be rightly pointed out that present day capitalism developed away from this condemned capitalism, and the same could be said for present day socialism. To suggest that whatever nowadays is called capitalism or socialism automatically comes under 19th century condemnations would betray a singular lack of subtlety.

What the traditional doctrine of the common good requires is that our defense of the capitalist system include the recognition of the primacy of the common good.   And indeed most defenses of entrepreneurial capitalism maintain that this system best insures the welfare of members of a society and that it is this that motivates the entrepreneurial capitalist.   Of course it will not do to say that there is some law according to which the greedy pursuit of wealthy results in the best for most others.   If this were merely the unintended accidental consequence of greed it cannot be introduced as moral justification.

What the traditional doctrine of the common good requires is that any defense of even a modified socialism include the primacy of the common good.   Not the collective good, not the greatest good of the greatest number, not some abstract criterion of particular acts no one knows how to apply.   The recent criticisms of Consequentialism must be taken into account by those who would defend even a modified socialism.

Our bishops are wise to see the defense of the family

as a fundamental concern, since if we do not learn of the
primacy of the common good in the family it is doubtful
that we will see it in the political and economic orders.
The good of the family is my good, one I share with
other members of the family, and it takes precedence
over my merely private good. I must love this shared or
common good precisely as shareable by many and if I
make sacrifices for it it is not because I put the private
goods of others above my private good. Rather, I
acknowledge the primacy of a good common to many
and more important than the individual or collective
private goods of the many.

It is because human persons are ordered to a variety
of common goods that the assertion of the primacy of
the common good can sometimes seemingly imply
unacceptable consequences. When Maritain wrote of
man as a person transcending the common good of
society, what he meant is not that in the crunch, *qua*
person, my private good takes precedence over the
common good. Rather his concern was with the
common good that transcends the common good of the
city, the supernatural end to which we are called. The
human person is ordered to God as to his happiness, his
ultimate end, his supreme good. But God is the
common *par excellence*. It is not the Catholic view that
human persons relate to God one-to-one, so to speak,
with God being *my* good in an exclusive sense. Indeed,
to love God merely as *my* good would be a defective
love. It would be to turn God into my private good, as if
there were commensurability between my finite will and
infinite goodness. The only appropriate way to love
God is as a good infinitely shareable. The rule of charity
makes this clear. I must love my neighbor as, like
myself, ordered to a common good.

The conception of the human person as chiefly and primarily perfected by common goods because he naturally and inevitably is a member of society, as opposed to the view of man as chiefly a monad whose good is a private one such that societal arrangements are for his private good although always diminishing it, has implications for political theory and for political economy. The doctrine functions as a guide or measure. It is not the case that one can simply deduce from such considerations the best political or economic arrangements. More likely than not, such principles can be embodied in a variety of arrangements whose desirability of preferability has to be decided on other grounds. But any economic or political system which collided with the primacy of the common good would be to that degree unacceptable from the point of view of the Catholic tradition -- and the truth.

SEVEN

LIBERTY IN THE CATHOLIC TRADITION

Vatican II's *Declaration on Religious Liberty* is often seen as a repudiation of the Church's traditional teaching on liberty and, more positively, as a belated adoption of the insights and advances of modern political theory. A comparison of Leo XIII's *Libertas* of 1888 with the *Declaration* of Vatican II, and indeed with Pope John XXIII's *Pacem in Terris*, lends credence to the view that Church doctrine has changed radically.

As for the second claim -- that the Church has fallen into line with modern political and legal thought -- this suggests a uniformity and clarity in modernism difficult to find.

In this essay, I want to recall aspects of Catholic teaching on human freedom, go on to say a few words about recent controversies among Catholics, and finally call attention to some of the profound theoretical problems which attend some modern views on human liberty.

The Biblical truth that God made man in His image has long been interpreted by theologians as meaning that man alone among earthly creatures can, like his creator, freely direct himself to the good. Thus, in the prologue to the second or moral part of his *Summa theologiae*, St. Thomas Aquinas uses the notion of man as God's image to establish the nature of man's moral agency: deliberate voluntary action.

Such action can be impeded in two ways, by ignorance and by violence. The freedom of an action is obviously affected if, for one reason or another, the agent does not know what he is doing. A large topic, needless to say, the discussion of which requires a distinction between culpable and inculpable ignorance. Traditional discussions of violence, on the other hand, immediately face a paradox. If the human act as such is self-generated, a forced act is not a human act. A forced human act thus appears to be logically impossible. Of course, a moral theory that had no room for violence would scarcely interest us. Room is made for it by distinguishing between the inner act of will and its execution. No one can force our consent, but we can quite easily be prevented from executing our choices and be carried hither and thither "against our will."

If the *Summa theologiae* be taken as a highwater mark of Catholic doctrine on human freedom, it can be said that its analysis of human agency continues to be held in respect by philosophers, both Catholic and non-Catholic. Alan Donagan's presentation of it in his contribution to the *Cambridge History of Later Medieval Philosophy* is a case in point.

But if the philosophical aspects of the traditional theory of human action are of continuing interest, in its theological dimension the theory goes beyond the dreams of mere philosophers. To the question "Why did God make you?" the *Baltimore Catechism* provided the crisp answer, "God made me to know Him, to love Him, and to serve Him in this world, and to be happy with Him forever in the next." In the Catholic tradition, freedom is *for* something. As God's image, it is man's task freely to direct himself to that which God has ordained as fulfilling of him. By contrast, other terrestial creatures are determined to their respective ends, though in the hierarchy of animal life, there is an intimation of freedom in the higher animals. On the Catholic view, the point of man's freedom is not to find the already written role he is to play in the drama of salvation. Rather, the end of human activity is given, but the articulation of that end and of the means of realizing it must be fashioned by the human agent. There is a common Christian vocation, but the Calendar of the Saints shows the all but infinite variety of ways in which it can be realized.

Man's end is to love God. Thus the fulfillment of his freedom is to be liberated from all that impedes that love, that is, to be freed from sin. This is the liberty of grace. Freedom from all obstacles to the attainment of our end is freedom from need and suffering. St. Bernard of Clairvaux developed the degrees of this freedom in his work *On Grace and Free Will*. It is, so to speak, by descending from this vision of man that a philosophical discussion of freedom takes place within the Catholic theological tradition.

By this I mean that the impetus to develop a theory of free human agency, and the motivation for interest in available philosophical discussions, is always found in man's true and complete end. It must never be forgotten that many of the key concepts of secular and philosophical discussions were developed by believers, thus exemplying the Anselmian adage *fides quaerens intellectum.*

When the Church discusses human liberty in a way meant to be intelligible to all, believers and unbelievers, she should not be taken to be entering the real world at last. The real world, man's true destiny, is the Christian vocation, salvation through Christ, eternal happiness with God. Any discussion of man that does not take into account man's true ultimate end may be true to some degree but is fundamentally inadequate. The Church's insistence on Natural Law is precisely an insistence on a common moral basis for discussion of human action. There are truths about human agents which can be grasped independently of Revelation. Nonetheless, from the Catholic point of view, discussions based only on such truths must seem exiguous. Moreover, apart from the sustaining context of religious belief, such natural truths can all too quickly fall into oblivion.

For all that, a common natural discussion is possible and my intention here is to give the wider context into which for the Catholic they fit. The natural discussion is carried on in terms proper to it. It is because natural truths cannot conflict with Revelation that the Church, despite her supernatural vision, insists on these common natural moral truths.

The notion that the Church has profoundly changed her doctrine on liberty and political freedom invites a first and obvious remark, namely, that Church teaching, taken broadly, consists both of abiding truths and contingent applications of them in different historical circumstances. The great historical event of modern times affecting both Church teaching and the attitude of individual Catholics is the French Revolution. Raised in a country that is itself the result of a revolution, we Americans are likely to have a positive, even a Hollywood, conception of the French Revolution. Serious positive assessments of it have come from such stalwarts of orthodoxy as Hilaire Belloc. But there was also a strong strain of intellectual resistance to and theoretical condemnation of the French Revolution by individual Catholics. The names of Chateaubriand, de Maistre, de Bonald and Donoso Cortes come to mind. What others saw as excusable excesses, these men saw as essential to the Revolution. The emergence of the modern secular state, of liberal democracy, which we instinctively regard as an unequivocal good, was seen as an attack on religion and on man's supernatural vocation.

But it was not merely individual Catholics who condemned the underlying political philosophy of the French Revolution. Its errors came to be gathered under the title of Liberalism which was condemned in various official Church documents, including Leo XIII's 1888 encyclical mentioned above. In French intellectual history, the famous condemnation of *Action Francaise* seemed to mark a radical shift in universal Church teaching.

Jacques Maritain, once more or less associated with *Action Francaise*, became an expositor of and apologist for the condemnation. For such theologians as the Jesuit Cardinal Louis Billot, the condemnation was a bitter blow. The chapter in his *De Ecclesia Christi* (Rome, 1929) entitled *De errore Liberalismi et variis eius formae: On the error of Liberalism and its various forms,"* sounds startling to Catholic ears only slightly more than half a century later. Surely the tone of Billot is utterly different from that of the Council Fathers in the early 1960's. Maritain, in his *Carnet de Notes*, recounts a visit made by the Dominican Garrigou-Lagrange to Billot that gives something of the flavor of that feisty man. Billot resigned as cardinal because of the condemnation of *Action Francaise*.

Maritain himself provides a good example of the opposed tendence that was to be expressed in the *Declaration on Religious Liberty*. The publication of the great French Catholic philosopher's *Integral Humanism* opened Maritain up to attacks from those who thought as Billot had. Maritain's Personalism was said to incorporate many flaws of the modern theory. In 1943, a controversy raged over Maritain's Personalism and its effect on the traditional doctrine of the common good. Maritain wrote *The Person and the Common Good* in order to clarify his position and, implicitly, to answer his critics. That is a long story, still awaiting its historian, but it connects with Maritain's fundamental effort, namely, to put together the traditional doctrine of Natural Law and the modern theory of Human Rights.

Earlier efforts culminated in *Man and the State*, the Walgreen Lectures delivered at the University of Chicago. The Declaration on the Rights of Man made in 1789 and 1793 are ringing generalizations that were very quickly used to justify the Terror, an historical fact that should give one at least theoretical pause. In 1948 came the International Declaration of the Rights of Man and it is precisely this document Maritain confronts in his Walgreen Lectures. The way he states the problem is of profound importance. The right to life, liberty and personal security seem beyond discussion, but of course they require a view of the human person and society to sustain them. It is just because there is no single social arrangement to confer such rights that Alasdair MacIntyre, in *After Virtue*, denies that there are any human rights in the sense desired. Similar misgivings were already expressed in the writings of Michel Villey. Maritain, while drawing attention to the various and conflicting views of man and society held by the signatories of the Declaration, attempted to show (a) that the true basis of them is Natural Law and (b) that the acceptance of the Declaration despite radically different ways of explaining and understanding it, suggested an implicit recognition of that true basis. More recently, John Finnis, in *Natural Law and Natural Rights*, has confronted the same issues. The work of these men enables us to state the difficulty attending the claim that the Church has belatedly accepted the modern view of political freedom and human rights. If the Church speaks of human rights in verbally the same way as others do, we must not take this to be an acceptance of the theoretical bases others might advance for such rights.

Guy de Broglie, S.J., in a little book published in 1964, *Le Droit Naturel a la Liberte Religieuse*, wisely discusses some of the issues in the then still pending conciliar declaration. His chief concern is to reconcile liberal and anti-liberal Catholics by arguing that the acceptance of the Declaration in no wise entails the false divinising of Liberty that the Church had previously condemned. Catholics who espouse liberalism favor the conclusions which follow from it, not its principles, which are antithetical to Catholicism. De Broglie does not think much of the inner coherence of the antigonistic theory and argues that its conclusions can be reached more surely from traditional Catholic principles. By presenting matters in this way, he hopes to establish a reconciliation between liberal and anti-liberal Catholics.

However forlorn that hope may seem, it can be said that de Broglie captures the essence of the Vatican II declaration. Rights familiar to many as flowing from principles antithetical to Catholicism are shown to follow from Catholic principles and are proposed to the faithful on that basis. De Broglie enables us to see why many thought the *Declaration on Religious Liberty* was a departure from past Catholic teaching and why, although there is some reason for their judgment, it is fundamentlly wrong. Just as Maritain could accept the 1948 Declaration only because he was able to produce a Natural Law justification of the rights claimed, so the Council Fathers could speak of liberty in terms familiar to modern ears only because they were able to found their talk of liberty in the traditional teaching of the Church.

Such efforts invite misunderstanding from friend and foe alike. Talk of human rights is of relatively recent origin and it developed in intellectual environments hostile to religious belief. The enshrinement of liberty was meant to be an act of defiance and we see all about us the problems arising from it. What cannot be overlooked is that modern talk of liberty and rights arose out of a view of the carrier of those rights which is both incompatible with Catholicism and wobbly on exclusively natural and philosophical grounds. The bearer of human rights is seen as an atom without a nature. His freedom does not flow from what he is and what he is for. It becomes a claim against other contrary free projects. The theory does not protect us from the interpretation that there is no right use of liberty, no uses which can be theoretically excluded as impermissible. All substantive claims about what man is and what he ought to do are taken to be subjective, mere opinions, such that to act on them in a way that affects others is unjust. Whether the view of society which arises out of the grouping of such atoms can be merely formal and still justify the merely formal or procedural concept of liberty, is a philosophical difficulty that cannot be wished away. Meanwhile, our laws and judicial decisions make mincemeat out of the residual substantive beliefs that were essential to the founding of the country.

Consider only the topic of the Vatican II *Declaration on Religious Liberty*. The history of the interpretation of the relation of Church and State shows a movement *from* non-establishment on a federal level *toward* judicial hostility to religion. Religious beliefs and practices are increasingly viewed as inimical to the secular state and are actively opposed as "divisive." Religious liberty has almost come to mean freedom from religion, with the state the instrument of the agnostic. That this is brought about by judges who hold religious beliefs suggests the danger for believers in accepting both the principles and the conclusions of their enemies. A faith that finds its foundation in symbols and parables would do well to be more wary of the modern tendency to flourish abstract terms. The rhetoric of liberty should not jeopardize the long theological tradition that developed a teaching on free and responsible human agency that still speaks to us today.

EIGHT

NATURAL LAW AND VIRTUE

If virtue is making a comeback in contemporary moral philosophy, the same cannot be said of natural law.

I think this is unfortunate. Indeed, it seems to me that our understanding of virtue will suffer fatally if we seek to separate virtue from the objective conditions in human nature which support it.

Much continues to be written on the subject of natural law, some of it excellent, but the very ascendancy of virtue carries with it the suggestion that to speak of human action in terms of law is to adopt an exiguous conception of persons. More seriously, there may seem to be a conflict between the natural law and virtue approaches to moral philosophy.

Iris Murdoch, in *The Sovereignty of the Good*, was one of the first to draw attention to the fact that the actor cast in the role of human person in the then dominant way of doing moral philosophy had little to do with flesh and blood individuals. The moral agent was thought of as someone facing a puzzle and seeking a solution to it, the suggestion being that getting clear about the problem and finding the solution to it summed up the ethical task. From this seemingly innocent assumption, odd consequences result.

First, the following disjunction presented itself. *Either* every waking moment is one in which the agent finds himself puzzled *or* the moral life is episodic. Since it is false that humans are forever confronting quandaries, the moral life, on the view in question, would be composed of those separate and discrete occasions when one is confronting a moral problem. But how is human life in the intervals to be described? As amoral or non-moral or what?

Second, the assumption that the moral life consists of events when the agent confronts a cognitive problem -- "What is the right thing to do?" -- predictably ran afoul of one of the oldest issues in moral philosophy. We cannot assume that *knowing* the solution *is* the solution. Nothing, alas, is more familiar to us than that we sometimes act against our best knowledge of what it is that we ought to do.

Knowledge and Virtue

The hope that knowing what we ought to do is tantamount to doing it dies hard. Socrates insisted that knowledge is virtue. The reverse of this claim is that acting badly is due to ignorance. Once ignorance is replaced by knowledge, it becomes impossible to act badly.

So ran the theory. And of course it ran aground on common human experience. The conclusion is inescapable. Important as knowledge is, it is not sufficient to guarantee good action. But if ignorance does not explain bad action, what does?

When Aristotle discussed the Socratic claim that to know what we ought to do suffices for doing it, he observed that it all depends on what we mean by "know." Someone napping on the lawn may know more nuclear physics than anyone else on the block, but presumably he is not presently considering it. Having knowledge and using it differ. So too someone can know something in general and not see its particular application. One might know that heat is soothing to an injury and not know that by doing such-and-such heat will be generated and comfort gained. Aristotle concludes that one can know something yet not be actually considering it, and know generally but not in particular.

Still and all, it may be wondered where such criticisms lead. What view of human agents could be substituted for that according to which we sometimes confront problems and have to solve them and use our minds to do so? It would seem very strange indeed to invoke Aristotle's authority against a position which stresses the fact that human persons are rational agents. Indeed, the mark of man, Aristotle observes, is that he acts according to reason and is good or bad insofar as he does this well or ill. True enough, but Aristotle also said that we do not become good by philosophizing.

It is not a question of denying that good behavior

involves correct thinking, but of asking what kind of thinking is involved. And one way of hitting upon the kind of knowledge on which good human action depends is by noticing the distinction between changing one's mind and changing one's life.

When Aristotle denies that knowledge is virtue, what he means is that the Fifty Drachma course from Protagoras is not just as such what will make us good. Abstract knowledge, what Cardinal Newman called "notional" thinking, does not engage us where we live. Newman contrasted the notion with the real. So too, Kierkegaard, another giant of the 19th century, contrasted Thought and Being, thinking and existing, but pointed out that existing, doing, acting, follow from another kind of thinking.

When in the *Nicomachean Ethics*, Aristotle confronted head-on the position Plato ascribed to Socrates in the dialogue *Protagoras*, he made an analysis of practical discourse. (He actually uses the phrase "practical syllogism", but then syllogism means discourse.) The discussion becomes somewhat technical, but the most striking element of it can be expressed as follows. The way we think as we act depends on the kind of person we are. That is, the thinking that guides our choice is essentially dependent on our moral character.

Like so many points made by Aristotle, this one is easily seen to be true. The reason we do not expect a coward to act bravely is that his way of assessing the circumstances in which he must act is colored by his past craven behavior. Isn't this what we mean by "rationalizing?" So too the sensualist sees the arena in which he must act through the lens of his disordered appetites. And, on a happier note, the brave and the just see the demands of courage and justice correctly because, to use the familiar phrase, their hearts are in the right place.

St. Thomas Aquinas develops this contrast in a way that exercised a great influence on, among others, Jacques Maritain. Imagine that you want advice on a matter pertaining to chastity, St. Thomas says. You might consult a moral theologian and he would speak to you generally but for all that say important and true things. He is not speaking *in propria persona*; indeed what he says is quite impersonal. He speaks with the authority of the knowledge he has, and the advice he gives, the judgment he makes, is, Thomas suggests, in the manner of knowledge *(per modum cognitionis)*. On the other hand, you might consult a chaste man who would listen to you, think a bit, and then begin by saying, "Well, what I would do..." He puts himself in your shoes and he sees the situation you have told him of with his own eyes, through his own character. He speaks in his own name and his advice reflects the bent of his character; he judges, Thomas suggests, by way of a kind of connaturality with the end in view *(per modum inclinationis)*. It is not that the moral theologian knows and the other man does not; rather, it is the different kind of knowledge each man has. And that of the man of experience is more proximately related to acts his listener might perform.

Like Aristotle, St. Thomas regards general knowledge of what we ought to do as valuable, but of little help when we act, since actions are singular and particular. Indeed, taken by itself, general knowledge of what we should do does not amount to much for the mind to lay hold of since it seems to be always in need of qualification -- "by and large" -- and, more importantly, of application. One does not need a moral theory in order to be good and one can have a moral theory without being good. Nonetheless, it is best to have both.

Natural Law

We can now state the opposition between natural law and virtue in a sharper way. Virtue (or its opposite) is that thanks to which we are what we are morally; furthermore, it is decisive for action in a way general knowledge is not. Whether virtue is moral or intellectual, having its seat in appetite or mind, respectively, it carries the imprint of reason. It is something we have (and thus is called a habit), it is our character, marking us as the moral type we are. Under its influence, correct choices are made easily, almost routinely. Habitual behavior is rational because it exhibits the rule of reason ingrained in appetites and inclinations. It is the existential realm of connaturality, of affinity and kinship with the known good.

As opposed to what? To general, disengaged, impersonal knowledge, notional thinking. And here's the rub for natural law. Natural law consists of the first, overriding, non-gainsayable principles or starting points of practical reasoning. These principles, accordingly, are not only general but most general, as general as you can get. "Do good and avoid evil." "Be brave." "Be just." "Act prudently." "Nothing in excess." I have stated them as commands because this underscores how little they help us in the crunch. The soldier in battle, wondering what to do, is not enormously helped by the command that he act bravely.

A man tempted in the way Graham Greene's Scobie is tempted in *The Heart of the Matter* is not immediately helped by being told he should be chaste. Of course, there are easily imagined circumstances where such general precepts would bear a quite particular interpretation. Kipling's reiterated "Be a man, my son," has specific content because of the contrasting behavior of others. But in and of themselves such common commands, by covering all possible cases, do not specify what I should do here and now.

Anyone who has read much about natural law will recognize here a standard criticism brought against it. "Do good and avoid evil?" Who would not accept that and contend that what he proposed to do is in keeping with the injunction? I propose to show how this feature of natural law, far from being a weakness, is precisely its strength (I do not say, its virtue).

The principles of natural law are often called precepts or commands on an analogy with the kind of things legislatures create. A law or statute is passed to govern behavior of a certain kind in a society. One is enjoined to act in one way rather than another, the injunction carries authority and punitive sanctions are attached. One might obey the law in order to avoid punishment, but that is scarcely a justification of the law itself. It would be an odd law that enjoined us to do something *in order to* escape punishment. What we are told to do could then be just anything. But ordinarily laws tell us to do quite specific things with the implicit reason that action of that kind will be conducive to the common good. That is, a law or precept orders us to take certain means either in order that the end of society be achieved or that it not be thwarted. The underlying model would thus seem to be end/means.

In classical times or the Middle Ages or a century or two ago, men spoke of the morally educative role of civil law. Laws enjoined actions which if not morally good were morally neutral and obedience to the law created the habits of the good citizen for whom the common good of the society took precedence over his merely private good, not because he feared punishment, but because the law helped him to become ordered to the common good as *his* good.

Many statues, of course, bear on matters which are morally indifferent, but the law elevates the indifferent to a moral status. Abstractly considered, there is no more reason to drive on one side of the road than the other; nonetheless, given the traffic laws, one has a moral obligation to obey them. Why? Because they aim at the common good.

Law and Natural Law

Sometimes there are laws which cannot be interpreted in this way. In a given society, the buying and selling of human beings may be legally condoned. In another society, the aborting of unborn children may have legal sanction. William Shirer, in *The Rise and Fall of the Third Reich*, devotes an entire chapter to a discussion of the care the Nazi regime took to make its practices, including genocide, a matter of law. Concentration camps, the incinerators at Dachau, were within the law. In all these cases, the critic will say that the laws in question are not aimed at the common good. He will say that these laws are unjust. He may even say that these laws are not laws.

Now clearly in some sense of the term even a bad law or an unjust law is a law. If it is enacted by the legislature or enunciated by the monarch, if it follows the legislative procedures of a given political regime, it is a law. To what then is appeal being made when it is said that a law is unjust or not really a law? At the Nurenburg trials there was talk of international law and this concept came under severe criticism. The world court and other creatures of the United Nations, to the degree that they depend on a notion of international law, may be open to the same criticism. The notion of international law, if it is taken to be the product of a supranational legislature, is a fiction. Consequently, courts which interpret international law would seem to be fictions too. (That they are often ideological instruments is another matter.)

This is not to say that countries do not bind themselves by treaties and even seek a third country to arbitrate differences, but this is not like appealing to federal law over state law or state law over municipal.

The Nurenburg trials were justifiable, not because some supranational body had passed laws that the Germany of Adolph Hitler violated, but because there is an unwritten law, known to all, and such Nazi practices as genocide, even if allowed by the laws of the Third Reich, were in conflict with *that* law. With moral law. With what from time immemorial has been called natural law.

"Law" is used here in an analogous sense. Of course, we think of legislatures when we hear the term; we are meant to. Only if we are clear about what we mean by "law" in this sense, can we grasp the extended sense of the term at play in such phrases as moral law and natural law. Natural law may be law only in an extended sense, but what it refers to is the measure of law in the ordinary sense. A law permitting murder is in conflict with the natural law injunction against killing the innocent; that is why it is an unjust law. To deny that it is a law at all, is not to claim it failed to meet certain procedural requirements, but that it enjoins action which would thwart the common good. When we appeal beyond the law, it is to natural law that we appeal.

Ethics and Natural Law

Individuals in making moral decisions are forming a judgment as to how they should act in these circumstances if a certain end or good is to be achieved. That judgment may be called a precept, as if the agent were issuing commands to himself, but of course it does not have the force of law nor is it incumbent on others to obey him.   This is already the case with the judgments of the moral philosopher. Say I write a book on moral philosophy in which I go on and on about what people ought to do in this area of action and that. You read the book and go on living as before without fearing that the McInerny constabulary, their uniforms reminiscent of the Swiss Guard, will show up on your doorstep with a warrant for your arrest. The charge? You have violated the principle laid down in Chapter Four of my book.

If the judgments of moral philosophers and the judgments of individuals as to what they ought to do do not have the force of law, they nonetheless have this in common with the precepts of law that they enjoin an action with an eye to attaining some end or seeing that an end is not thwarted. Thus the end/means analysis is common to law, to ethics and to individual practical reasoning. That is why it was once all but universally held that the mark of a human action is that it is an undertaking for the sake of some end.   That is, of any human action whatsoever it can be said: it is for the sake of some end.

Just as natural law is of importance when questions arise as to the status of civil law, so it is of importance when the question arises as to whether or not there is any objective standard of human moral judgments. The legal positivist holds that a society can make any law it wishes and that the law it makes is a law and that is the end of the matter. There may be procedures within a society for changing laws as well as making them, but while a law is a law it is quite simply a law. On this view there is nothing to prevent a society from legalizing genocide, abortion, homosexuality, child abuse, and so on.

Surely it is one of the profoundest ironies of our day that while the Nazi genocide, under the label of the Holocaust, has become an almost universal symbol of unequivocal evil, legal theorists of the positivist persuasion argue that the Nazi laws were no less laws than the prohibition of mass murder in other societies. But to say that a moral objection to law leaves the law as such untouched is to trivialize the moral condemnation.

It was not all that long ago that an analogue of legal positivism was imported into ethics by R. M. Hare. Like Aristotle and Thomas, Hare saw moral discourse as a search for means to an end. Such discourse would seem to be reducible back into common overriding principles, and Hare agreed. His reader was somewhat surprised to learn that, according to Hare, by all accounts a good and decent man, one might hold the extermination of Jews as his principle. Thomas and Aristotle would have said that such a principle is a bad one, a false one, an erroneous one, but Hare did not feel such talk is justified. If someone held that all Jews ought to be exterminated and continued to hold it even if he discovered that he himself was Jewish, then nothing more can be said. The principle passed the only tests Hare knew for a principle to be a moral principle, such formal tests as universalizability. There is no way to assess or appraise or rank or condemn moral principles as such, nor does there seem to be any substantive reason for holding those we do. The principles we hold are held on the basis of feeling, inclination, whatever, what Hare called a "Decision of Principle"; there is no objective, realist defense of them possible.

Universal Emotivism

Far from maintaining a unique position, Hare could be said to have expressed rather precisely a common assumption about moral judgment and moral disagreement. We might engage in a rational discussion about how we and others ought to act on the assumption of some goal or principle, but if the principle itself comes under question, the discussion stops. There are irreducibly different points of view. Radically different opinions. I see it one way and you see it another. I can reason within the assumption of a point of view, a principle, an end, but I cannot maintain that it would be false to say that the pursuit of an end contrary to this one is fulfilling of the kind of agent we are.

Notice what is not being said. It is not a matter of pointing out how difficult it is to change other people's minds and how even more difficult it is to get others to change their lives. Emotions get in the way, commitments, personal history. All that is true but leaves open the question whether a given course of action can be argued to be incompatible with the kind of agent we are. It might be hard to change a Nazi's mind but that does not mean it is impossible to argue that genocide is wrong.

Secondly, there are all kinds of compatible objectives and goods and ends that humans pursue. ' This agent cannot pursue a given end and its opposite, but it may well be that either end is a good one. Moral realism in the form of Natural Law does not commit one to the view that in any given set of circumstances there is one only course of action that could justifiably be performed. Not at all. It is part and parcel of the Natural Law tradition that the moral life is all but definable as actions performed according to practical judgments that are only for the most part binding. Most moral advice is tentative precisely because there is not a single right thing to do in given circumstances. It falls to each moral agent to fashion his particular path through life.

What Natural Law maintains is that there are objective parameters of our moral life, that at the limits of moral discourse there are some few principles or precepts which hold not just for the most part, usually, but always. This is clearer in the case of negative precepts. We are never permitted to kill the innocent. Stealing is always wrong, and so is lying. Fornication and adultery can never be done licitly. And so on. But the moral ideal which consists of temperance and courage and prudence and justice is not optional. It is true of every human agent that he should be just, temperate, brave and wise.

Earlier we mentioned that it is a familiar complaint against Natural Law that it does not tell us what specifically to do. It does not. Some actions are conducive to justice and others thwart it, but most judgments about how we should bring about the end of justice do not deal with means without which justice could not be achieved. The moral task is to apply the ideal to ever changing circumstances. Of course Natural Law, which consists of the most common principles, does not tell us how to apply them here and now. The fundamental importance of Natural Law is to show the impossibility of the kind of radical relativism positions such as Hare's involve. If MacIntyre is right in maintaining that Emotivism characterizes modern moral philosophy, and emotivism is untenable, I suggest that Natural Law is involved in the effort to show it is untenable.

Let us say that, in speaking of a proposed course of action, you say it is the thing to do, meaning the moral thing to do, and I strongly disagree, saying it is wrong. Your judgment takes the form "X is good" and mine the form "X is bad" and X stands for the same thing. What you might mean is that doing X fits in with your vocation or plan or goal and my disagreement might then mean that you are wrong to think that getting an MBA will advance your career as a pole vaulter. Let us say that there are things to be said on both sides and there is really no knock-down-drag-out way of resolving the issue.   This sort of disagreement happens all the time; it is of the essence of conversation. We may think that there are better reasons for the one course of action than for its opposite, but usually we recognize that there are *some* reasons on the other side. Furthermore, one need not be a pole vaulter nor even have an opinion about how advancement -- or elevation -- can be gained in that pursuit. No ethical theory should promise to help us find the one and only course of action in any circumstances whatsoever.

What seems to be widespread today is the notion that there are irreducibly different outlooks or standpoints which lead to different notions of what is right or wrong, good or bad, and that we simply cannot discuss these outlooks. We cannot say that one outlook is bad because to say this is to say it from another outlook. When adopted as a radical position, this relativizes moral judgments, and leaves one theoretically without resources to declare that genocide is wrong. (I am assuming that any moral theory that cannot give reasons why genocide, murder, theft, etc. are wrong is a radically deficient moral theory, indeed is a moral theory only in the way a bad law is a law.) "X is good" may be true from your point of view and false from mine. Fair enough when the value of X is pole-vaulting; pernicious when the value of X is genocide. Not only is it pernicious to hold this in the case of genocide, it is also incoherent. How?

The Incoherence of Relativism

To say that all judgments are relative is to get involved in something like the Liar's Paradox. If your judgment that all judgments are relative applies to itself, then it does not apply to my judgment that all judgments are not relative. If it does not apply to itself, then it is false. One dislikes this kind of refutation because it has an excessively tricky sound to it. Nonetheless, the only appropriate way to handle a verbal denial of the undeniably true is to show that the negator cannot consistently maintain his position. Such a *reductio* is not meant to establish the truth of anything so much as to make it clear that some truths are so fundamental they cannot coherently be denied.

Very well. It cannot be universally true than each and every moral judgment is relative to a standpoint one may or may not adopt. (A further feature of Emotivism, remember, is that the adoption of standpoints or principles is irrational and thus not susceptible of justification.) However hospitable moral discourse is to relative judgments -- most moral judgments are relative, true only by and large if true at all -- fundamentally, at its limits, moral discourse reposes on judgments that are necessarily true and self-evident in the sense that one cannot coherently deny them. What principles are these?

Obviously, to see that universal moral relativism is incoherent does not as such inform us as to what the moral absolutes are. But then we do not begin thinking about the moral life from such an abstract and formal perspective. Moral philosophy is a special reflective instance of the thinking we engage in when we act. In acting we are sorting out possible courses of action, weighing and appraising them, choosing the one that in the circumstances seems to us best conducive to the end in view. We have at least implicitly adopted a notion of what the human good is and how it can be obtained. This is why Plato and Aristotle begin by wanting to clarify the nature of human happiness, the human good, the ultimate overriding end. They attempt to free from the particularities of this action and that the embedded implicit notion of the human good. Human agents make decisions as members of families and societies and sometimes as mere individuals and it was clear to the Greeks that a human being could attain the fulfillment that is implicitly pursued in any action only as a citizen and member of a family. "Man is by nature a political animal."

That is the essential note of the Natural Law. We must fashion our lives with free and responsible choices and the area left to our own devising is, abstractly speaking, almost total. Nonetheless, there is the given of our nature to provide a remote guide. If we are naturally political, there are numberless morally legitimate ways in which society can be organized. Natural law is a constraint in the sense that it makes it clear that we cannot speak of the human good if we do not think there is any human nature to be brought to fulfillment. What is fulfilling of the nature that is ours is temperance, courage, justice and practical wisdom. "Be temperate" may not tell me what to do or not to do here and now, but it provides an ultimate criterion of assessment. To assert that intemperance, cowardice and injustice are the human good is not simply an undiscussable alternate viewpoint. It is an untenable because incoherent position. Genocide is not simply in conflict with *my* outlook (but just fine from a Nazi point of view); it is a perniciously false claim about what is fulfilling of the kind of agent we all are.

It will be seen that Natural Law is not a position one puts forward as following from something else and provable in that way. The precepts of Natural Law are those no one can fail to know, at least in this sense that attempts to hold their opposites lands one in self-contradiction. Natural Law has this feature in common with other first principles. One does not prove the Principle of Contradiction; rather one shows that the denial of it can only be verbal. (If A = [p . -p], then -A is as true as A, and one has asserted nothing.) So is it analogously with the starting points, principles, of practical reason. We do not try to persuade someone that he should seek the good. We do not honor the claim that the human good has nothing to do with reason -- any attempt to show that to be true exhibits its recognition of the centrality of reason. In much the same way we deal with claims that murder is sometimes right, that stealing and lying are in certain circumstances permitted, and so on. Natural Law is proved by showing that seeming alternatives to it are incoherent.

I began by suggesting that, welcome as is virtue's return to prominence in moral philosophy, it stands in need of the supporting doctrine of Natural Law. The reasons for that suggestion will now be clear.

Virtue or character is a settled disposition or habit thanks to which we easily and quickly appraise the

fleeting situations in which we find ourselves in the
light of an end or good that is *ours*, a good with which
we have affinity and connaturality because of our past
history of pursuing it. We are inclined and ordered to it,
cognitively and appetitively, and this enables us to
recognize opportunities that would not otherwise be
clear to us. Not to have a virtue is not to be in a neutral
condition. Every agent has a personal history thanks to
which he has the character and habits that are his. He
may have acted in such a way that he is unjust,
intemperate, cowardly. He is thereby inclined to see the
situations in which he finds himself in the light of ends
he has long pursued. If he is unjust, he will be blind to
the demands of justice in a concrete situation. If he is a
coward, the opportunities of brave action will not even
occur to him.

If something like this is true, moral character seems to
relativize action is a fairly decisive way. It is at least a
partial reason why we sometimes find others
unintelligible and sense that they find us the same. Their
way of looking at things is simply not ours and it is as
difficult for them as it is for us to rise above our outlook.
Oftentimes, most often, these differences are morally
legitimate and testimony to the freedom with which
men can pursue the good indicated by their common
nature. But when a parent tells his child he must not lie,
he is not merely passing on "his values," imposing on
the poor child his own viewpoint. No more do
lawgivers consider that they are imposing their own
viewpoint when they prohibit murder. The case against
murder is not that it is incompatible with what
lawgivers think: rather, it is incompatible with the
human good. Lawgivers must think that truth to act on
it, but it is not their thinking it that makes it true.

Of both the virtuous and the vicious it can be said
that, thanks to their character, their freedom has been
modified, as well as their ability to see things from the

other's point of view. In some sense, they may have nothing to say to one another. When they do talk, the proponent of virtue is painfully aware that, however telling his arguments, it is unlikely the other will be changed by them. "One does not become good by philosophizing." In short, we may seem to have here all the elements that have led to radical moral relativism. That is why it is important for the proponent of virtue to recognize that the denial of the good he seeks does not have equal status with its affirmation. Furthermore, the denial cannot consistently be maintained.

What is the relation of Natural Law to habitual virtue? Its most important role is in distinguishing those habits which are virtues from those which are vices. Unless the great ends of action are appropriate to the agent, are what is good for him, the rule of reason ingrained in appetite will guarantee that we act badly rather than well. Thus it is the humble but important function of what is called Natural Law to say obviously true things about moral agents, to sketch at a level of great universality the constituents of the human good, and thereby state the limits of moral discourse, to show the moral skeptic that his position is untenable and to enable us to see that the personal, connatural thinking that is embedded in action reposes ultimately on general principles whose enunciation is occasionally a matter of great practical importance.

If virtue is the personal appropriation of the good sketched in the precepts of Natural Law, Natural Law provides the ultimate basis for seeing our common humanity in a way that celebrates the inexhaustible legitimate differences exemplified in virtuous acts.

NINE

MARITAIN AND NATURAL RIGHTS

Readers of Alasdair MacIntyre's *After Virtue* will have been struck by an apparent inconsistency. On the one hand, he says that Maritain is someone from whom, in the immediate past, he has learned much, presumably on the subjects addressed in the book. [*After Virtue*, Notre Dame University Press, p. 242] On the other hand, one of the key arguments in this excellent book is that natural rights are fictions.

The difficulty can be sharpened. It is well know that Jacques Maritain regarded the United Nations Universal Declaration on Human Rights as a landmark. His attitude toward that world body reflects the optimism and enthusiasm common during the first years of the United Nations. In the speech Maritain gave to the second international conference of UNESCO in Mexico City, published in 1947 as *La Voie de la Paix*, Maritain gave expression to views to be further developed in his 1951 book *Man and the State*. By way of contrast, here is MacIntyre.

In the United Nations declaration on human rights of 1949 what has since become the normal UN practice of not giving good reasons for *any* assertions whatsoever is followed with great rigor. And the latest defender of such rights, Ronald Dworkin, in *Taking Rights Seriously* (1976), concedes that the existence of such rights cannot be demonstrated, but remarks on this point simply that it does not follow from the fact that a statement cannot be demonstrated that it is not true... Natural or human rights, then, are fictions -- as is utility -- but fictions with highly specific properties. (ibid, p. 67)

My aim in this chapter is to look at Maritain's remarks on human or natural rights from our end-of-the-century viewpoint to see how precisely he admitted the doctrine of natural rights into his political philosophy and to see whether he has provided defenses against the kind of criticism of rights talk MacIntyre has developed.

Nothing comes more easily to a Thomist than to notice that in recent centuries much has been lost in ethical and political theory that is essential to the fashioning of a doctrine of rights. When Maritain called for an end of Machiavellianism, he insisted that classical and medieval moral and political thought are meant to apply to men as they are, to fallen men, men of flesh and blood. To dismiss classical and medieval thought as the idle idealizations of the underemployed about a world that never was is a libel against them. As practical philosophy, such theory is meant to be action guiding. *Realpolitik* on the other hand cannot be described as taking men as they are and trying to lead them to the good. Rather it is a matter of accepting evils and trying to turn selfish interests, whether of individuals or groups, to public benefit.

Thomistic moral and political philosophy addresses man in his totality -- what he is, in the sense of his failures and faults and sinfulness; what he can and ought to become, in terms of the teleology of his nature, of his role in creation.

Prima facie, one would expect a Thomist like Maritain to be in profound sympathy with MacIntyre, to agree with him about what he calls the Enlightenment Project, and to insist that modern theory is so denatured that it has no basis on which to erect a doctrine of rights. Surely it would be odd in the extreme to cast Maritain in the role of defender of the Enlightenment or indeed as the defender of any of MacIntyre's main targets. Students of Maritain will think immediately of *Moral Philosophy: An Historical and Critical Survey of the Great Systems*. Nonetheless, Maritain does defend the modern doctrine of natural rights, with specific reference to the UN declaration. Looking into this paradoxical situation will reveal it to be even more complicated than these opening remarks suggest.

Les droits de l'homme et la loi naturelle, published in 1941, provides a good starting point for our inquiry. After a moving passage in which he argues that the currents of liberty and fraternity opened by the Gospels, the virtues of justice and friendship sanctioned by them, their emphasis on the human person and authority's ultimate answerability, provide the internal energy thanks to which civilization can reach its fulfillment, Maritain adds:

Those who do not believe in God or who do not profess Christianity, if they nonetheless believe in the dignity of

the human person, in justice, liberty and love of
neighbor, can also cooperate in the realization of such a
society, cooperate for the common good, though they be
unable to trace their practical convictions back to first
principles or base them on deficient principles. (p. 177)

Maritain wrote this by way of commentary on the
fourth of the four characteristics he feels are essential to
a society of free men: that it be personalist,
communitarian, pluralist and theist or Christian. He is
not laying out a plan for a theocracy or for a
government that could only be realized by believing
Christians. He is speaking of the only kind of society
befitting free human beings. Such a society, he says,
must be theist, even Christian, in the sense that there is
recognized in it the dignity of the human person, justice,
liberty, love of neighbor and so forth, *on whatever basis
these be held.*

That basis may not be the only adequate and sufficient
one, the derivation of all creation, man included, from
God, but may be some basis short of yet dependent on
that or -- this is what is extraordinary -- a basis of
deficient principles.

Such criticisms of modernity as MacIntyre makes
argue from the deficiency of the principles from which
natural rights are derived to the conclusion that the
resultant rights are fictions, a criticism which reaches its
apotheosis when confronted with the blithe admission
that natural rights cannot be proved at all. Anyone who
has been impressed by the opening sweep of chapters in
After Virtue may fear that, by contrast, Maritain's
assumption that universal consent to the four
characteristics of society can be easily gained is empty
and inane. *Can a theory antithetical to Maritain's own
theism ground the same natural rights?* It is to Chapter IV
of *Man and the State* that we must turn for a discussion of
this fundamental issue.

The first section of that chapter bears as title the ringing assertion: *Men mutually opposed in their theoretical conceptions can come to a merely practical agreement regarding a list of human rights.* This section opens with the remark that we nowadays have come to a fuller realization of a number of practical truths about human life than out forbears, and it is this alleged progress in realization that has gone hand in hand with a divergence in theoretical conceptions (which depend on ideological allegiance, philosophical and religious traditions, cultural backgrounds, historical experiences). He takes the Universal Declaration of 1948 to be proof that men can, with whatever difficulty, achieve a common formulation of such *practical conclusions* which are "the various rights possessed by man in his personal and social existence."

> Yet it would be quite futile to look for a common *rational justification* of these practical conclusions and these rights. If we did so we would run the risk of imposing arbitrary dogmatism or of being stopped short by irreconcilable differences. The question raised at this point is that of the *practical agreement* among men who are theoretically opposed to one another. (p. 76)

Although indispensable, he continues, rational justifications are powerless to create agreement among men. They are indispensable because everyone believes instinctively in the truth and wishes to give consent only to what is true and rationally valid. The powerlessness of theoretical justifications to create agreement is attributed to their plurality and the backgrounds out of which the plurality of justifications arise.

Maritain recognizes that he is holding a paradoxical position. Let us be clear about the difficulties it involves. There are certain practical judgments,

judgments about what should be done, on which all men can agree despite the fact that they have radically different ways of justifying those judgments.   A MacIntyre would suggest that such radical diversity affects the very meanings of the judgments and thus makes the agreement merely verbal.   Unfortunately, Maritain gives no examples here and I will not attempt to provide one lest it skew the discussion.   He notices that the UN Rights of Man Declaration commanded agreement from the various signatories *provided we are not asked why*. "With the 'why', the dispute begins." (p. 77)

At this point, Maritain quotes his UNESCO address cited earlier.

> How is an agreement conceivable among men assembled for the purpose of jointly accomplishing a task dealing with the future of the mind, who come from the four corners of the earth and who belong not only to different spiritual families and antagonistic schools of thought? Since the aim of UNESCO is a practical aim, agreement among its members can be spontaneously achieved, not on common speculative notions, but on common practical notions, not on the affirmation of the same conception of the world, man and knowledge, but on the affirmation of the same set of convictions concerning action. This is doubtless very little, it is the last refuge of intellectual agreement among men. It is, however, enough to undertake a great work; and it would mean a great deal to become aware of this body of common practical convictions. (pp. 77-78)

Men do not share a common speculative ideology or common explanatory principles, but "when it concerns, on the contrary, the basic *practical* ideology and the basic principles of *action* implicitly recognized today, in a vital if not a formulated manner, by the consciousness of free peoples, this happens to constitute *grosso modo* a sort of common residue, a sort of unwritten common law, at the point of practical convergence of extremely different theoretical ideologies and spiritual traditions." (p. 78)

Now this may sound extremely strange to us. It may seem to do little more than recall those halcyon postwar days when it was possible to look upon the United Nations with hope. The decades since have taught us that the language of rights puts a weapon into the hands of those for whom words have meanings diametrically opposed to those we understand. The Soviet Union is a signatory of the Universal Declaration and its understanding of human rights is opposed to our own not simply on the level of theoretical ideology and explanatory principles, but precisely in the practical order, as witness the Soviet Union's backing of a resolution to declare Israel guilty of genocide. Maritain's "last refuge of intellectual agreement" seems to be as well the last refuge of scoundrels.

> To understand that [common practical agreement], it is sufficient to distinguish properly between a rational justification, inseparable from the spiritual dynamism or a philosophical doctrine or religious faith, and the practical conclusions which, separately justified for each, are, for all, analogically common principles of action. I am fully convinced that my way of justifying the belief in the rights of man and the ideal of freedom, equality and fraternity is the only one which is solidly based on truth. That does not prevent me from agreeing on these practical tenets with those who are convinced that their way of justifying them, entirely different from mine and even opposed to mine in its theoretical dynamism, is likewise the only one that is based on truth. (p. 78)

But the problem is, what will 'freedom,' 'equality' and 'fraternity' mean, and mean practically? Maritain sees the agreement that produced the Universal Declaration as pragmatic, not theoretical, and feels that nothing "prevents the attainment of formulations which would indicate notable progress in the process of world unification." (p. 79)

This makes sad reading some thirty years later. The pragmatic agreement has been a snare and a delusion and it would seem naive to deny it. To the degree that Maritain's teaching here is linked to the fact of the UN, it will seem to have been pretty well weakened if not completely refuted by history. There has been, in other words, a pragmatic disproof of his pragmatic agreement.

Does this mean that, since MacIntyre is surely right about the Universal Declaration and Maritain is surely wrong, that we must agree with MacIntyre that the notion of common human rights is simply a fiction? Perhaps not. The Church speaks to us again and again in terms of the rights of all human persons and regards these rights as natural; that is, while the reminder comes to us from the teaching Church, while our convictions about such rights shares to a degree in the certainty of our divine faith, *what* we are being reminded of, *what* we are certain of, are rights that can be naturally recognized. Let us go further: *there are natural rights that are actually recognized by men.*

What I want to do in the remainder of this paper is to develop a version of Maritain's linking of natural rights and natural law which will enable us to see the defensibility of his teaching on these matters.

Maritain makes quite clear in *Man and the State* what the correct theoretical foundation of the doctrine of natural rights is. It is quite simply the natural law, properly understood. (p. 80) There may be competitive theoretical or ideological explanations put forward in justification of natural rights, but for Maritain only one of them is the true one. Furthermore, if it is true, it will provide an explanation of how it can be that, despite the plurality of theoretical justifications, there can be agreement in the practical order, and of course I mean a plurality of theoretical justifications in and of the practical order. Just as the theory of natural law is a theory which is both in and about the practical order, so presumably are the other justifications Maritain refers to.

In putting forward a sketch of natural law here, Maritain makes his famous distinction between the first element of natural law, which is ontological, and the second, which is gnoseological. Not a very promising distinction, you might think, since if law is as such *aliquid rationis*, it would seem always to be gnoseological and never merely ontological.

By the ontological element of natural law Maritain means man's nature in virtue of which he possesses ends which necessarily correspond to his essential constitution and which are the same for all. Every natural and artificial thing has a nature in the relevant sense, but man is endowed with intelligence and determines his own ends and must put himself in tune with the ends necessarily demanded by his nature.

> This means that there is, by virtue of human nature itself, an order or a disposition which human reason can discover and according to which the human will must act in order to attune itself to the essential and necessary ends of the human being. The unwritten law, or natural law, is nothing more than that. (p. 86)

But what precisely is the ontological element of natural law? "the *normality of functioning* which is grounded on the essence of that being: man." (p. 87-88)

The second element of natural law, the gnoseological, is "natural law *as known*, and this as measuring in actual fact human practical reason, which is the measure of human acts." (p. 89) The only practical knowledge all men have naturally and infallibly in common as a self-evident principle, intellectually perceived by virtue of the concepts involved, is that we must do good and avoid evil. But this is not so much natural law as its principle or preamble. "Natural law is the ensemble of things to do and not to do which follow therefrom in *necessary* fashion." (p. 90) However, every sort of error and deviation is possible in the determination of these things.

Another distinctive note of Maritain's understanding of natural law is the contention that it is an instance of knowledge through inclination. (p. 91)

It is of course tempting to want to worry over the niceties and details of even so swift a presentation of the doctrine of natural law as we find in Chapter IV of *Man and the State*. On another occasion I might succumb to that temptation, but not on this one. I shall end this chapter by attempting to state, *a la* Maritain -- who of course develops his own views *a la* St. Thomas Aquinas -- a resolution of the seeming paradox of his position.

What again is the paradox, not to say the seemingly insuperable difficulty, of what Maritain so often says in connection with such documents as the Universal Charter?

On the one hand, there is the fact that a great many signatories have surprisingly agreed to the declaration of human rights.

On the other hand, there is the fact that they would put forward different and even incompatible justifications of the rights listed, justifications which may vary from inadequacy to outright untruth.

But is it possible to separate the understanding of the rights, and the sense of the agreement, from the explanations and justifications that are given of them?

Natural law precepts beyond Do Good and Avoid Evil, even though they express ways of acting necessarily connected with the ends of human nature, are formulated only with difficulty, with much veering and careening and intermittent error.

In what sense of 'same' could the same precepts be formulated on the basis of radically different theoretical assumptions?

Maritain would say that we have difficulties because we are thinking about the *gnoseological* natural law. But surely any declaration of rights would pertain to the gnoseological and that is the area where differences are rife.

The only hope for Maritain's position would seem to be this.

The verbal agreement on a list of human rights which are justified theoretically in many and incompatible ways is founded, not on those different justifications, but rather on what Maritain calls the ontological natural law.

This means, I take it, that even inadequate and false justifications have embedded in them an implicit recognition of the true ends of human nature and thus of the true basis for practical precepts.

As a theory, natural law may be one theory among others. But if it is a true theory, there must be certain truths about the practical order that no man can fail to know. Nonetheless, men say and thus apparently think that ways of action incompatible with precepts of natural law are permissible.

This does not mean that when someone thinks that the direct killing of the innocent is sometimes justified, he *really* thinks the exact opposite. What it does mean is that such a personal already knows that which will show his judgment to be wrong.

The preamble and principles of natural law are already implicitly known by every human agent. The means of refuting our erroneous moral judgments are already possessed by us and are indeed latent in the process whereby we make the erroneous judgments.

This means that the verbal acceptance of the rights of man, while it may in a given case profess to be based on grounds that are false, can be grounded on bases already implicitly known by the one making the erroneous judgment.

If I judge that the direct killing of the innocent is sometimes permitted, I am judging that such an action will be fulfilling and perfective of the kind of agent I am. The fundamental criterion of my judgments is the human good, what is perfective of the kind of agent I am. In the example, I have mistakenly taken a certain kind of action to be conducive to that good or to be an articulation of it. If then I can be made to see that actions of this type are always and everywhere inimical to the human good, destructive of it, *I already have a basis for changing my mind.* Changing my ways is a different and more difficult matter, but until and unless I come to see that my practical judgment is actually inimical to the good I had thought it conducive to, existential change cannot occur.

Whether or not this is equivalent to Maritain's distinction between the ontological and gnoseological elements of natural law, it is certainly similar to it. My distinction is perhaps better described as one between implicit and explicit knowledge of natural law. But is my distinction sufficient to explain the agreement among signatories of wildly different outlooks on a list of human rights? I do not think so. I am not sure that Maritain has succeeded in giving a satisfactory explanation of that agreement either -- that is, succeeded in showing that it is indeed an agreement that goes beyond mere words which have radically different meanings for different signatories.

An agreement which must accommodate the kind of ideological cleavage that obtains between the West and East seems necessarily empty. The history of the United Nations since Maritain wrote cannot be ignored. Decades of experience on the part of truce teams, arms talk teams, human rights commissions, cannot be ignored. Helsinki accords which are largely ignored indicate that there are quite different notions of what even the word 'agreement' means. An agreement that is not one of substance, assuring the same meaning of the same words and the same scheme of justification, is no agreement at all. There is no shortcut to such agreement. As MacIntyre suggests, the Universal Declaration resides on a fiction.

Nonetheless, there is embedded in the very disagreements the possibility of agreement. Call it the ontological natural law, call it the implicit knowledge of natural law precepts which is compatible with explicit knowledge in partial variance with them, human persons can come to agreement on human nature and human rights, but only on the basis of the truth.

The Roman Catholic has a powerful reminder of the reality of human rights in innumerable documents of the Ordinary Magisterium as well as in the documents of Vatican II. One need not be a believer to recognize those rights, however practically necessary it is for fallen man to have that supernatural bolstering of natural knowledge. But the non-believer must understand the true basis of those rights in human nature or it is not human rights he is recognizing.

TEN

ART AND CONNATURALITY

Owing doubtless to the bifurcated influence of contemporary thought, which is engaged on the one hand in bloodless analysis and on the other in an impassioned voluntaristic emphasis on the nonintellectual, Thomists have of late been taking a great deal about connatural knowledge. Indeed, in the encyclical Humani Generis, Pope Pius XII saw in connatural knowledge a refutation of the claim that Scholastic thought does not pay sufficient attention to the role appetite plays in knowledge.

Never has Christian philosophy denied the usefulness and efficacy of good dispositions of soul for perceiving and embracing moral and religious truths. In fact, it has always taught that the lack of these dispositions of good will can be the reason why the intellect, influenced by the passions and evil inclinations, can be so obscured that it cannot see clearly. Indeed St. Thomas holds that the intellect can in some way perceive higher goods of the moral order, whether natural or supernatural, inasmuch as it experiences a certain "connaturality" with these goods, whether this "connaturality" be purely natural or the result of grace; and it is clear how much even this somewhat obscure perception can help the reason in its investigations. (n. 34)

In what follows, I will first examine the meaning of connatural knowledge in the moral order and then St. Thomas's use of the term "connatural" in other contexts. Then I will try to see why, if the notion of affective connaturality is to be extended to the realm of art, one must distinguish between the habit of art and poetic knowledge, as Jacques Maritain has done.

1. *Judgment and Connaturality*

In the three texts of St. Thomas Aquinas most often referred to when the question of connatural knowledge arises, we find him talking about judgment as the act of the wise man. There are two kinds of wisdom and consequently two kinds of judgment. With regard to what is to be done, there are two judgments which are relevant. The one is that which can be given by one who possesses moral science. Such a man can judge about virtuous acts even if he himself does not possess virtue; he has a cognitive grasp of ethical matters and judges *per modum cognitionis.* Another type of judgment in moral matters is that made by the virtuous man who may or may not have learned moral science. When he judges that is to be done, he is involved in a more than cognitive way, since he is inclined toward what ought to be done by the virtues he possesses. His judgments is said to be one *per modum inclinationis. (ST, Ia,* q. 1, a. 6, ad 3m)

It is this second kind of judgment that St. Thomas, in another text (*IIaIIae.*45.2), calls a judgment based on connaturality with the things to be judged.

> Dicendum quod sicut supra dictum est, sapientia important quamdam rectitudinem iudicii secundum rationes divinas.   Rectitudo autem iudicii potest contingere dupliciter: uno modo, secundum perfectum usum rationis; alio modo, propter connaturalitatem quamdam ad ea de quibus iam est iudicandum. Sicut de his quae ad castitatem pertinent, per rationis inquisitionem recte iudicat ille quid didicit scientiam moralem; sed per quamdam connaturalitatem ad ipsa recte iudicat de eis ille qui habet habitum castitatis.

The first kind of judgment, that *per modum cognitionis,* is correct   because of a perfect use of reason.   The rectitude of the judgment based on connaturality is due to something other than intellect.   It must be kept in mind that the act of judging is always an act of intellect; it is not that something other than the intellect makes the judgment when connaturality is spoken of, but rather that the rectitude of the intellect's judgment is due to something outside the intellect itself.

The emphasis in the above mentioned texts is on practical wisdom and ,what is alluded to as connaturality is brought out by St. Thomas in his analyses of the judgment of prudence, which he calls human wisdom (*sapientia viro,* quoting Proverbs 10:23 (*IIaIIae.*47.2.1m) As *recta ratio agibilium,* prudence is an intellectual virtue. Unlike science, however, prudence is concerned with contingent and variable matters in their very contingency and variability -- with what is to be done here and now in these particular circumstances. The prudential syllogism has as its major a rather universal proposition, grasped in a purely cognitive way, *intra limites intellectus,* in Cajetan's phrase *(In IamIIae*.58.5); for example, that the goods of another ought to be returned. What prudence must do is see particular circumstances in the light of this common principle. The common principles which serve as the major premiss of prudential syllogisms may be drawn from the diligent inquiries of moral science or may be something absolutely of natural law. But however the major is had, what is of interest here is the minor of the prudential syllogism.

How will prudence judge in this particular case when it is a question, say, of this borrowed book, whose permanent retention would be a desirable thing? One can accept the universal statement that what belongs to another should be returned; in an ethics class one may find it relatively easy, within the confines of a fictive case, to apply the principle to "particular" circumstances. But now, here and now, what is the person's judgment about returning this borrowed book? He is involved in the judgment of the here and now, and the history of his past actions, the kind of person he is, enters into the reckoning. *Qualis unusquisque est, talis finis ei videtur.* The judgment of the particular circumstances which is the minor of the practical syllogism, depends for its rectitude on the appetitive condition of the person who is to act. The judgment is *extra limites intellectus* in the sense that the appetite influences the judgment of reason. What is required here and now is not theoretical truth but practical truth. (*QD de virtutibus in communi*, a. 6, ad 5m.)

The truth of the speculative intellect is quite in keeping with the movement of the intellect relative to things. The intellect is said to be true insofar as it is in conformity with the way things are, and the properly cognitive mode consists in the assimilation of things to the intellect. The intellect is said to receive things, not in the way in which they exist in themselves, but rather in its own immaterial mode. In order for a material thing to be known intellectually it must be separated from the mode belonging to it as it exists, that is, from its materiality and consequent singularity. Intellectual knowledge is abstractive, immaterial, universal. Appetite, on the other hand, tends towards things as they are in themselves. We love things for what they are and in themselves; not as we know them but as they are. We could thereby say that the mode of appetite is more existential than that of the intellect. (Cf. *In de Divinis nominibus*, cap. 2, lect.4) Something of this conformity with things as they are in themselves, of this existential mode, is present in the notion of the practical truth of the prudential judgment.

Prudence is an intellectual virtue, but a virtue of the practical intellect which seeks knowledge in order to operate. Since prudence is concerned with human affairs, it is to the end of man that it directs individual actions. As is always the case when something is to be done, the end is the beginning. (Aristotle, *Ethics* 1151a16) The end of man is something given insofar as it follows on the nature of man. This end is something which is known naturally. *(IIaIIae.47.6)* The considerations of prudence, its judgments and its command, must presuppose this end and the rectification of appetite relative to this end.

> Consequently it is requisite for prudence, which is right reason about things to be done, that man be well disposed with regard to ends; and this depends on the rectitude of his appetite. Therefore, for prudence there is need of moral virtue which rectifies the appetite. *(IaIIae.57.4)*

It is because the intellect cannot conform to the particularity and contingency of singulars that the judgment of prudence cannot be true with speculative truth. But it is precisely singulars which must be judged when it is a question of commanding an action here and now. From the point of view of cognition, only opinion could be had about singular contingents as singular and contingent. And yet I must make the right decision. The rectitude of my judgment, accordingly, must depend upon something other than intellect.

> On the other hand, the truth of the practical intellect depends on conformity with right appetite. This conformity has no place in necessary matters, which are not effected by the human will, but only in contingent matters which can be effected by us... *(Ibid.*, a. 5, ad 3m)

The truth of the prudential judgment depends upon rectified appetite, appetite determined to the end or good. And since appetite, as mentioned above, moves toward things as they are in themselves, as they exist, appetite assimilates one to what is desired; one becomes like what one loves, becomes connatural with it. It is precisely this connaturality which is characteristic of appetite that makes the prudential judgment, which depends upon appetite, a judgment by connaturality or inclination. Moral science, because its consideration of *agibilia* does not entail appetite *(In VI Ethic.* lect. 7, n. 1200), judges *per modum cognitionis.* It is precisely the influence of appetite on the prudential judgment of *agibilia* that makes this judgment one *per connaturalitatem.*

2. *Virtue and Appetite*

The judgment through connaturality, as it figures in the texts cited, is such because of a special dependence on appetite. Why is it that the influences of appetite on the object of intellect makes the judgment connatural? If this is not answered, we shall encounter great difficulties when we find St. Thomas speaking of the habit of principles as proceeding *per modum naturae*. An even greater difficulty arises when we read that the *habitus* of geometry induces a kind of connaturality with the geometrical. If we speak of connaturality in these last two cases, we are clearly not speaking of affective knowledge. It is imperative therefore to examine the scope of the term "connatural" in St. Thomas if we are to avoid calling the most perfectly scientific knowledge affective.

In Aristotle's *Ethics* [1106b10; *In II Ethic.*, lect. 6, n. 315; *Q.D. de veritate*, q. 10, a. 10, ad 9m] one reads that moral virtue is more certain than science. The reason given is that moral virtue inclines in the same way nature does, that is, by determining the appetite to one   object. Virtue is generated by accustoming the appetite to a certain mode of operation by repeated acts; this custom becomes a second nature which determines the appetite to one object. (*QD de virt. in com.*, a. 9) Far from settling anything, however, this raises more questions. The intellect too is the subject of habits, of second natures, and because of these virtues the intellect too is determined to one. Is not determination to one what distinguishes science from opinion?

First of all, we must ask what meaning of certitude is at play in the remark that moral virtues is more certain than art or science. This is a puzzling claim because certitude is something we should tend to restrict to reason and science. *Moral* is derived from the Latin *mos* which has a two fold signification. Sometimes it signifies custom; at other times it signifies a natural or quasi-natural inclination to do something. "Now *moral* virtues is named from *mos* in the sense of a natural or

quasi-natural inclination to do some particular action."
(*IaIIae*.58.1) The second meaning of *mos* is of course
close to the first since custom is a second nature and
gives an inclination similar to that of nature. What is
more, the inclination spoken of belongs most properly to
appetite. With regard to certitude, it is well to recall the
distinction St. Thomas makes between certitude
simpliciter and certitude *secundum quid*. The first,
absolute certitude, is taken from the cause of certitude;
certitude in this sense has degrees insofar as its causes
are more or less determined. Certitude *secundum quid* is
that taken from the part of the subject, and in this sense
what is most perfectly proportioned to intellect is most
certain. (*IIaIIae*, q. 4, a. 8) This distinction is reducible to
another St. Thomas makes, that between the motive for
adhering to a truth and the evidence for the truth. . (*QD
de veritate*, q. 14, a. 1, ad 7m)

What seems to emerge then is this: Moral virtue is
said to be more certain than art and science because it
gives a more perfect determination to one. Why is this?
It is nature in the sense given in Aristotle's *Physics*
which is first of all the principle of determination to one.
(*QD de malo*, q. 6, a. 1) In the *Physics*, nature which
always acts in one way is distinguished from the
principle of rational acts. (*In II Physic*, lect. 13, ed. Pirotta
n. 503). Reason is said to be *ad opposita* and not *ad unum*
(*In IX Metaphysic.*, lect. 2, nn. 1789-93), even when it is
the subject of habits. For example, the physician in
knowing health knows its opposite, sickness. The
explanation of the *ad opposita* is based on a difference
between intellect and will already mentioned and
indicates why will better saves the *ratio naturae*. It is
because intellect receives things in its own mode that
oppositions in things do not preclude intellect's
possessing opposites. Appetite, on the other hand,
relates to things as they exist, and in existence the
presence of one thing *eo ipso* excludes its opposite. Thus

appetite is more *ad unum*. (*QD de caritate*, a. 6, ad 8) A further indication that will is more like nature than is intellect is found in the fact that the former moves as an efficient cause and the latter as a formal cause. (*IaIIae*, q. 9, a. 1, ad 3) That nature is an efficient cause is seen in its *ratio propria*. (*In II Physic*. lect 1, n. 194; *In X Metaphysic*. lect 5, n. 810)

What we have already seen in the analogy of the word *nature* can also be seen by an analysis of the analogous word *virtue*. The definition of virtue given by Aristotle in the second book of the *Ethics* is "that which makes the one having it good and renders his operation good." Given the recurrence of "good" in the definition as well as the fact that good is the object of appetite, it is difficult to see how we can speak of intellectual virtues. In addressing this difficulty, St. Thomas points out that the reference to the good required for virtue can be either formal or material. (*QD de virt. in com.*, a. 7) A potency is formally related to the good when it bears on it precisely as good, something only appetite can do. A power can be related to the good materially when it bears on a good but not under the formality of goodness. Thus, those habits which have appetite as their subject, or which depend upon appetite, are most properly virtues. Those habits, on the other hand, which are neither in appetite nor dependent upon it, can refer materially to the good and be, in a certain sense, virtues. With this as background, St. Thomas goes on to discuss intellectual virtues.

> Both the speculative and practical intellect can be perfected by habits in two ways: first, absolutely and as such, insofar as their acts precede will and move it in the line of formal causality; secondly, insofar as their acts follow on appetite as commanded and elicited by it. Habits generated by acts of the first kind are less

properly virtues, since they do not bear on the good
formally as such. *Intellectus*, science, wisdom and art are
virtues in this sense. (ibid.)

These habits only render the subject capable of
operating in a certain fashion; there is no disposition of
appetite relative to the good which is consequent on the
possession of these habits. In the classical phrase, they
make one able (*potens*) but not willing (*volens*). (*Ibid.*)

Those habits of the speculative and practical intellects
which follow on the will are more truly virtues, for by
them one is made not only capable of acting correctly
but also willing to. St. Thomas shows what he means by
analyzing faith and prudence.

By faith, the intellect operates *per modum naturae* and
intellect is not moved by its proper object as in the case
of science. Rather, in faith, one assents "through a
choice of the will turning to one side [of a contradiction]
rather than the other." (*IIaIIae*, 1, 4) Will enters into the
very specification of the object of faith, and not merely
in the line of efficient causality. (QD de virt. in com., a.
7) John of St. Thomas has written some very
illuminating pages on the role the will plays in the
assent of faith. The will, he says, can add nothing to the
apprehension of the object, to its evidence, but it can
render it pleasing. Moved by the will (under the
influence of grace, of course) determining its object, the
intellect assents to the truths of faith because they are
pleasing. (*Cursus theologicus, In IIamIIae, de fide*, disp. 3,
vii) *Nemo credit nisi volens.*

Prudence, a virtue of the practical intellect, does not
depend upon the will for the determination of its object
but only for its end. Given the will's ordination to the
end of man, prudence seeks the means of attaining this

end. We have already seen the dependence of prudence on moral virtue in making its judgment.

An indication of the difference between faith and prudence on the one hand and *intellectus*, science, wisdom and art on the other can be seen in the fact that a man does not lose the habit of science by not knowing certain truths which pertain to that habit. In the case of faith, however, while faith remains, one cannot believe anything contrary to faith. The reason given is that science inclines *per modum rationis*, whereas faith inclines *per modum naturae*. (*In III Sent.*, d. 23, q. 3, ad. 3, sol. 2, ad 2; *IIaIIae*.1.4.3m)

These different habits participate in the *ratio virtutis*, then, in this order: first, moral virtues, then such intellectual habits as faith and prudence, and finally and least properly *intellectus*, science, wisdom and art. So too with regard to the way in which they imitate nature and incline *per modum naturae*, the same order obtains. Appetite takes priority over intellect in imitating nature; and habits which have appetite as subject or which depend in a special way upon appetite will incline *per modum naturae* more properly than purely intellectual habits.

In the light of this, it should no longer surprise us to find St. Thomas using the notion of connaturality to speak of knowledge which is in no way affective. *Connatural* means "in accord with nature," and since *nature* means many things, so too will *connatural*. Thus in speaking of geometry, St. Thomas says that, once a person possesses the science, its objects become connatural to his intellect. It is important to avoid identifying *connaturality* in such a context with its use in the texts mentioned at the outset of this chapter. And of course it is knowledge through affective connaturality that most Thomists have in mind when they speak of connaturality.

What are the advantages and disadvantages of judgments by affective connaturality with an object? In the practical order, we can see that, for better or worse, the condition of appetite exercises a decisive role in the operative syllogism. *Qualis unusquisque est, talis finis ei videtur.* In the theoretical order, custom, connaturality, reason led by custom, is indispensable at the outset of the intellectual life -- and an abiding danger as well. At first one assents to the truth *quia placens* or because he believes in his master. *(In Boethii de trin.,* lect. 1, q. 1, a. 1) In either case, appetite enters into the very specification of the intellect's object. But the intellect should eventually proceed *per modum rationis* and assent because of the evidence of the object proposed. The danger of custom in the intellectual life is pointed out by Aristotle at the end of the second book of the *Metaphysics.* (Cf. *In II Metaphysic.,* lect. 5) One may *want* the poets cited as authorities or he may *want* a mathematical procedure in metaphysics because he finds these familiar and pleasing.

When things are beyond the comprehension of our intellects, affective connaturality assumes a new and awesome importance. We have seen in the remarks of St. Thomas and John of St. Thomas the role which the will plays in the assent of faith. The evidence of its proper object being insufficient to bring about the assent of intellect, the will moved by grace prompts assent. This assent is not absurd, for the intellect could not assent in this fashion to something which contradicts what it certainly knows. So too in the gift of wisdom, the influence of the will perfected by charity proportions divine things to the intellect, makes it connatural with them so that one judges sapientially, referring everything to God.

3. *The Virtue of Art*

Our analysis of texts has indicated somewhat precisely the role the will plays in connatural knowledge. We will now go on to see why the notion of judgment by affective connaturality or inclination does not apply to the habit of art.

A virtue, we have seen, is a quality which makes the one having it good and renders his operation good. Or, as it is also expressed, that which gives not only the ability, but also the inclination, to act well. It is the central position of good as the object of virtue which led St. Thomas to distinguish between virtues properly so called and those habits which are less properly virtues. There is no question here of judging their respective worth, dignity or desirability. Rather, it is a matter of unequal participation in the *ratio virtutis*. In analogous names, that which most properly saves the *ratio nominis* is not always the most perfect *in re*. Now, since the good enters in a very special way into the *ratio* signified by the word "virtue," and since goodness is the proper object of appetite, those habits will most properly be called virtues which have appetite as their subject or which depend in a special way upon appetite. The intellectual virtues of faith and prudence were seen to depend upon appetite as preceding the proper act of reason, and thus they were said to be properly virtues. Of the acquired virtues, *intellectus*, science, wisdom, habits of the speculative intellect, and art, a habit of the practical intellect, were said to be least properly virtues. The will can move these virtues as an efficient cause insofar as their objects are included under the common notion of the good, but these four habits are of themselves only materially related to the good. (*QD de virt .in com.*, a.7)

What is of interest here is that art is aligned with the habits of the speculative intellect rather than with prudence when it is a question of how art saves the *ratio virtutis*. (*IaIIae*.57.3) Art does not make the one possessing it a good man' rather it makes him capable of judging correctly what ought to be done if the artifact is to be good. *Perfectio artis consistit in iudicando.* (*IIaIIae*.47.8) In order that a man *use* art well, his appetite must be rectified by moral virtues. (*IaIIae*.57.3.2m) Just as in the case of the speculative habits, it does not matter whether the artist is angry, sad or elated when he operates; the artifact can still be well made. The vices of the artist are no less vices, but they do not necessarily affect his art. An indication of the fact that the perfection of art is in the judgment is the frequently quoted remark of Aristotle that the artist who intentionally makes a mistake is better than one who does so unintentionally. In prudence, however, it is less wrong to err unintentionally than intentionally. (*IaIIae*.57.4; *IIaIIae*.47.8) Since judgment is proper to intellect, it would appear that art is more intellectual than prudence. Not depending on appetite as does prudence, art does not rely on the rectification of appetite relatively to the end of man. Moral virtues are necessary for the good use of art, but that is all. (*IaIIae*.57.1) This is but another indication of art's affinity with the habits of the speculative intellect.

Thus far it would seem that connaturality, an intrinsic dependence upon appetite, has nothing to do with art any more than it has with the habit of first principles or with science. And yet to settle for this would be to overlook the rather important fact that art is a virtue of the practical intellect. And the practical intellect, unlike the speculative, does not seek knowledge for its own sake but with a view to operation. And whether the operation is doing or making, the role of the will would seem to be somewhat more central than in speculative knowledge. What is more, St. Thomas tells us that art is true with practical truth, and practical truth is the intellect's conformity with rectified appetite. (*IaIIae*.57.5.3m)

On the one hand, St. Thomas has said that art like science and wisdom, is not dependent on the rectification of appetite. On the other, he applies the notion of practical truth -- a judgment in conformity with rectified appetite -- to art. How can these two affirmations possibly be reconciled?

Cajetan, in commenting on the article in question, devotes the bulk of his treatment to art and practical truth. What distinguishes the practical from the speculative, he argues, is not knowledge but the fact that the practical directs. (*In IamIIae*.57.5, n. II) The truth of the direction of the practical intellect must always depend upon rectified appetite. However, Cajetan would distinguish two meanings of rectified appetite in order to maintain the difference between art and prudence. The truth of the direction of the practical intellect in *agibilibus* is dependent upon conformity with appetite rectified with regard to man's end. The truth of the direction of practical intellect in matters of art, on the other hand, is dependent upon appetite rectified relatively to the end of art. Cajetan warns the novice in these matters not to confuse the truth of the direction of art with the use of art. Direction and use coincide in the production of the artifact, but they remain formally distinct. (*ibid.*, n. IV)

The difficulty that arises is this: What manner of rectification of appetite is required by art? In prudence, this rectification is had by the possession of the moral virtues, having appetite as their subject. Cajetan has made clear that it is not the moral virtues which give the rectification of appetite that art requires. Does this rectification require virtues at all? If not, why speak of rectification? If so, precisely what virtues are they supposed to be? A glance at the artistic process as described by St. Thomas dissipates these difficulties.

St. Thomas distinguishes three steps in the actual direction of art.(*QD de ver*. 4.1) Presupposed by this actual direction are a great many things, of course: the knowledge the artist might have, his experience of life, and so on. But in the actual direction there is first of all the *intentio finis*, reason proposing to will the artifact to be made. The next step, the *excogitatio formae*, is the judging of the means necessary to realize the proposed end. It is here, as we have seen, that the perfection of art lies. Now, the question we are asking is this: Since the judgment of the means will be true by practical truth -- that is, in conformity with rectified appetite -- what is required on the part of appetite for this rectification? We have already seen that it does not require the rectification which follows on possession of the moral virtues. (John Of St. Thomas, *Cursus theologicus, In IamIIae*, disp. 16, a. 4)

The end of art is contained in the exemplar idea which is present in the mind of the artist. The end of art, unlike that of man as man, is not *in affectu* as by the moral virtues. (*QD de ver*. 4.1) The judgment of the means of attaining the opus is not dependent on the condition of the appetite as is the judgment of prudence. St. Thomas's solution of the difficulty is succinct and simple. The will does not require any habitus to perfect it so as to relate it to the end proposed by art. (*QD de ver*. 5.1) The appetite does not need any virtues to bring it more surely under the control of art; the judgment of art, therefore, is not affected by appetite. This is why St. Thomas places art with the speculative virtues and not with prudence. This is also why we cannot say that the judgment of art is one by affective connaturality.

4. *Poetic Knowledge and Connaturality*

Although no one has maintained that the judgment of art is connatural, it has been held that poetic knowledge -- as opposed to and presupposed by art -- is a type of connatural knowledge. In a chapter already lengthy, it would not do to attempt a detailed analysis of these views. Ours will be the much less ambitious task of seeking in metaphor, which is the proper instrument of the poet, evidence of connatural knowledge.

If, as we have tried to show, the judgment of the means of realizing the idea, which is the proper act of the virtue of art, does not lend itself to the notion of connaturality, it seems that the creative or exemplar idea does. One can be said to judge connaturally when appetite moves the mind in the order of formal causality, coloring and inclining that which specifies the intellect: when *affectus transit in conditionem obiecti.* (*Cursus theologicus, In IIamIIae,* disp. 18, a. 4) When a truth which is above the comprehension of the intellect is presented for assent, the will, under the influence of grace, can render the truth, not evident or intelligible, but pleasing. The consequent assent of the intellect is due to a specifying activity of appetite. Could one derive from this the general rule that whenever a connection is not sufficient to move the intellect in the proper line of evidence and truth, appetite can formally influence the judgment by rendering the connection pleasing.

Poetry is said by St. Thomas to be concerned with things which do not have sufficient intelligibility to force the assent of the intellect. (*In I Sent.*, *prolog.*, a. 5, ad 3; *IaIIae*.101.2.2m) It is because of the lack of truth and cogency that poetry is said to need metaphors in order to seduce reason into assenting. This last remark may be a sign of something which had preceded the poem in the experience of the poet. When one reads *Dover Beach*, he is presented with a judgment on man's relation to the universe. Without hazarding an exegesis of the poem, it could be said that the net conclusion is that one's beloved is the sole refuge in a deluding, malevolent, even irrational, universe. Stated as baldly as this, the idea is not much, but of course that is not how Arnold present the idea. Appeal is not made directly or solely to the mind; rather, the images and rhythms of the lines get into our viscera and emotions and the "argument" is rendered pleasing and acceptable. If we accept *Dover Beach* it is not *quia verum est* but rather *quia placens*

This is hardly revolutionary. Neither does it seem forced to say that Arnold, by writing the poem, is allowing us to share in a way he once looked at things. And just as our experience in reading his poem is not an exercise in pure reason, neither, we can surmise, was the experience which the poem conveys a totally rational one. (Some might say "more than rational" but this suggests something other than quantitatively more, as if what were meant is "better than rational" or suprarational. Poetry may be more human than science, but it is for all that *infima doctrina*.)

If one takes a rather broad view of metaphor as a seeing of things in terms of other things, one might imagine the poet finding a pleasant *collatio* (later to be expressed in metaphor) to which his intellect can assent.

The likening of his love to a rose surely does not appear to the poet as a thought charged with intelligibility and yet, in the very confusion of the comparison, there is that which appetite can transform into something pleasant.   The expressed metaphor would result, presumably from a judgment of the virtue of art. How best express the collation that has been rendered pleasant? The answer to this question, it would appear, is found in a rational search for the best verbal expression for the previous confused connection in the poet's mind.

It would seem that it is something like this that is intended when poetic knowledge is spoken of in terms of affective connaturality. We have seen that, if one is desirous of applying such connaturality to the realm of art, he must attach it to something other than the virtue of art. Perhaps some such appetitive connaturality is involved in the knowledge of the poet; nevertheless, there would seem to be a more profound and more traditional way of speaking of the knowledge of the poet as connatural, this time using the term to signify something other than the influence of appetite on the judgment of intellect. One thinks of the phràse, *poetae nascuntur*, poets are born, not made. If it is true that a poet is born such, that his physical make-up (not to be understood superficially) and his imagination are especially apt for finding surprising similitudes among things, then his knowledge would be connatural in a much more basic sense of the term. Is this why Aristotle speaks of a gift for finding metaphors, an inborn gift (*ingenium*), not to be learned, following on the very nature of this man who is a poet? (*Poetics* 1459a5)

Whatever of these two ways of extending the notion of connaturality to poetic knowledge be chosen, it is certain that there is no place for affective connaturality in speaking of the direction of the virtue of art. Whatever the explanation of it, it is delightfully true that the poet can come upon the world in a grain of sand and render this collation, if not less unlikely, nevertheless pleasingly cogent.

ELEVEN

MARITAIN AND POETIC KNOWLEDGE

It could be said that the philosophy of art has had as little influence on its ostensible subject as the philosophy of science has had on its. Thus it is noteworthy that Jacques Maritain's reflections on art and poetry, which span his long active career, not only were inspired by a profound involvement with art and artists but also influenced a number of artists when they reflected on their own efforts. To cite a single instance, Flannery O'Connor, in the letters selected by Sally Fitzgerald under the title *The Habit of Being*, often acknowledges her debt to *Art and Scholasticism*.

What precisely was it that O'Connor learned from Maritain? It seems that the basic negative lesson was that art is not self expression.

> Also to have sympathy for any character, you have to put a good deal of yourself in him. But to say that any complete denudation of the author occurs in the successful work is, according to me, a romantic exaggeration. A great part of the art of it is precisely in seeing that this does not happen. Maritain says that to produce a work of art requires 'the constant attention of the purified mind,' and the business of the purified mind in this case is to see that those elements of the personality that don't bear on the subject at hand are excluded. Stories don't lie when left to themselves. Everything has to be subordinated to a whole which is not you. Any story I reveal myself completely in will be a bad story. (p. 105)

Art as a virtue of the practical intellect whose end is the *bonum operis*; the good of the thing made is a notion Maritain got from Thomas Aquinas who got it from Aristotle. It came to Flannery O'Connor as a fresh wind. It both confirmed her own hunch and influenced her later work. But the passage she puts in quotation marks is one that any student of Maritain will recognize as what is most distinctive about the great French Catholic philosopher's views on artistic knowledge.

Maritain once said that he would prefer to be seen as a Paleo-Thomist rather than as a Neo-Thomist. He was steeped in the thought of his master -- *Vae mihi si non thomistizavero* -- but like all genuine disciples he was a creative follower, extending the insights he found in Thomas into areas undreamt of by his mentor. This is nowhere more evident than in the uses to which Maritain put the concept of judgment by connaturality he found in St. Thomas. Maritain's analogical prolongation of connatural knowledge from its Thomistic setting into the realm of poetic knowledge not only provides a topic central to Maritain's aesthetics but also a good test case of his style of creative Thomism.

I what follows, I shall recall the Thomistic doctrine, developing it in the settings St. Thomas himself did, and then go on to consider Maritain's extension of connatural knowledge to poetry, emphasizing first how the analogy limps and then its essential fruitfulness. My first task involves some rather technical discussions but in pursuing it I will keep technical language and scholarly folderol to a minimum. A basic way of pursuing the second task would be to pursue the chronological development of Maritain's thoughts on the matter, singling out the persistent strands, drawing attention to aspects which emerge only gradually and later. This will not be my approach here. Rather, assuming without proving the essential unity and consistency of Maritain's thoughts on this matter, I will blend together a number of sources with an eye to giving the strongest possible presentation of his thought.

I

In the First Question of the First Part of the *Summa theologiae*, where St. Thomas is setting forth his conception of theology, the question arises as to whether theology can be characterized as wisdom. The third objection in Article Six suggests that theology cannot be called wisdom because it is acquired by means of study whereas wisdom is an infused gift of the Holy Ghost. Thomas's reply to this objection caught Maritain's eye and planted a seed that was to bear an immense fruit.

> Since judgment pertains to wisdom, wisdom will vary as types of judgment vary. In one way, a person judges by way of inclination, as one who has the habit of virtue rightly judges the things that are to be done according to that virtue insofar as he is inclined to them: that is why it

is said in the *Nicomachean Ethics*, Book X, that the
virtuous man is the rule and measure of human actions.
In another manner, [a person judges] by way of
knowledge, as someone instructed in moral science can
judge the acts of a virtue even if he does not possess the
virtue. (*Summa theologiae*, Ia,1.6.ad3m.)

As is well known, the *Summa theologaie* was intended
to be an introductory work but, since the neophyte in
theology is supposed to be already instructed in
philosophy, preliminary discussions of theological issues
often ride on brief reminders of what is already
presumed known from philosophical study.   The
remarks St. Thomas here makes concerning the
judgment of the virtuous man and the judgment of the
man learned in moral matters the moral philosopher, is
meant to remind his reader of what he has learned from
the study of such works as Aristotle's *Nicomachean
Ethics*. Let us recall some of those presuppositions.

The reader of the *Ethics* is not someone on the
threshold of the moral life; he comes to this work of
philosophical reflection against the background of his
personal history of acting. Human action, by definition,
is rational behavior, so the presupposition of moral
philosophy is an experience which has a cognitive
component. Anyone who acts knows what he is doing:
for a human being to act is to act consciously. This is not
to say, of course, that any human agent has a *theory* of
human action. We may even ask if one needs the kind of
reflection moral philosophy is in order to act well. The
answer is surely negative. Moral philosophy is not a
requirement for good human action. On the contrary, it
could be argued that unless there were instances of
good human action, moral philosophy would have no
empirical base on which to build. It would be an odd
claim that without three credits in ethics one could not
become a good man. "One does not become good by

philosophizing," Aristotle observes and, in the passage referred to by St. Thomas, Aristotle says that with respect to human actions the virtuous man is a rule and measure. The moral philosopher is guided in his reflections by noticing the way good men behave.

Moral action involves a judgment as to what is the good or fulfillment or perfection of the agent as well as judgments as to how that good can be achieved in fleeting and changing circumstances. A more sobering Aristotelian observation is that most men are bad. The fact that every human person after a certain age is willy-nilly engaged in the moral life obviously does not entail that everyone is acting well. This suggests a kind of paradox. Were we to select at random a human agent -- it might be ourselves -- the statistical probability, if Aristotle is right, is that we will have selected a bad man. Nonetheless, the agent we have chosen will be such that, besides that in him which explains why he is going wrong, there is also some intimation of what his good really consists in.

Moral philosophy as practiced by Aristotle is the effort to sort out the judgments latent in human action and appraise or assess them in the light of principles which are also latent in them. The aim of moral philosophy is not simply to attain theoretical knowledge of human action, but to provide guidelines which enable the agent to act well in the future. Moral philosophy thus appears as reflection on the level of generality which takes its rise from particular human deeds and seeks to close the circuit by being helpful in future action. That is what is meant by calling it practical knowledge. Its ultimate aim is not the perfection of the mind, but the perfection of action, choices, decisions.

On the assumption that happiness is a term anyone would accept as designating the point of acting at all,

Aristotle argues that most men seek their happiness or fulfillment where it cannot really be found. Once true happiness has been clarified, the moral philosopher is in possession of his most powerful tool for determining the kinds of action conducive to or destructive of human happiness. That is the basis on which he gives his general advice. It is the generality of moral philosophy which is its *grandeur et misere*. Clarification of what we ought to do is an achievement but, being general, it cannot immediately apply to the singular circumstances in which we must act. True, the moral philosopher can develop cases, tell stories of typical human acts, but these are meant to range over many instances and there remains the problem of application. Moral philosophy cannot by itself close the circuit mentioned earlier.

The judgment of the moral philosopher is a purely cognitive one; it does not as such engage his subjectivity. That is why, as St. Thomas points out, the moral philosopher can speak of the demands of a virtue he does not himself possess. The recognition that the judgment embedded in the singular act is not purely cognitive leads to the distinction between kinds of judgment. By moral upbringing, by the study of moral philosophy, or even without it, I act in the light of more or less articulate notions of what one ought to do in circumstances of a given kind. What happens when my action is not in conformity with my knowledge?

Let us say that I know I should be temperate in the consumption of alcohol. I may be a veritable poet of temperance and yet, alas, regularly overindulge and later feel remorse. My defective action does not seem to follow from a cognitive defect. I know what I ought to do, yet when I overindulge I *decide* to do so, I *judge* that here and now it is good for me to have yet another drink. Knowledge is in conflict with knowledge, judgment with judgment. The singular action or decision will be in conformity with the principle when the good expressed in the principle is *my* good, which my appetite is habitually inclined to it.   This is why St. Thomas speaks of the singular moral judgment as true by conformity with rectified appetite: that is, with the appetitive orientation to the true good.   If I am appetitively inclined to what is not my true good, my purely cognitive recognition of the true good cannot be efficacious in action.

Perhaps this can suffice as a gloss on the passage from the *Summa theologiae*. Any singular moral judgment is a judgment by way of inclination and it will be a good one if I am inclined to what is my true good.   If we ask advice of a good man who is not also a moral philosopher, his answer, after reflection, is likely to take the form, "Well, what I would do is..." That is, he puts himself in our shoes and judges in accordance with his steady orientation to the true good.   The advice of the moral philosopher, on the other hand, does not thus depend on his own moral condition.

The judgment by appetitive inclination or, as it is also called, affective connaturality, has its natural habitat in the analysis of singular moral decisions.   Thomas himself extended it to discussions of the assent of faith as well as to judgments made under the influence of the Gift of Wisdom.   In the primary instance, will or appetite has a steady inclination to the true good thanks to the possession of habits of virtue. That is why the virtuous man is the measure in human action. In the case of faith, it is the will prompted by grace that moves the intellect to assent.   Judgments made under the influence of the Gift of Wisdom presuppose an appetitive orientation. But nowhere does St. Thomas apply judgment by inclination or connaturality to the realm of art.

II

Not only does Thomas not speak of a judgment by way of inclination or affective connaturality in the case of art, there seem to be good reasons why he would not have done so. Prudence or practical wisdom is the virtue of the practical intellect thanks to which a person judges well as to what will make his actions, and himself, good, and this judgment, in order to be efficacious, depends upon the possession of moral virtues, that is, on a steady appetitive orientation to the true good. The aim of prudence is to make the human agent good. Art, on the other hand, is a virtue of the practical intellect whose aim is the good or perfection of the thing made. Prudence is concerned with doing (*agere*) and art with making (*facere*). Maritain, in *Art and Scholasticism*, Chapter III, develops the contrast between them.

> Art. which rules Making and not Doing, stands therefore outside the human sphere; it has an end, rules, values, which are not those of man, but those of the work to be produced. This work is everything for Art; there is for Art but one law -- the exigencies and the good of the work. [*Art and Scholasticism and The Frontiers of Poetry*, translated by Joseph W. Evans, Notre Dame University Press, p. 9.]

The sequel to this passage may well be what Flannery O'Connor found so liberating in Maritain's presentation.

> Hence the tyrannical and absorbing power of Art, and also its astonishing power of soothing; it delivers one from the human; it establishes the *artifex* -- artist or artisan -- in a world apart, closed, limited, absolute, in

which he puts the energy and intelligence of his manhood
at the service of a thing which he makes. This is true of
all art; the ennui of living and willing ceases at the door
of the workshop. [*ibid.*]

Maritain is here being guided closely by St. Thomas
Aquinas. In speaking of art as a virtue (*recta ratio
factibilium*), Thomas stresses the independence of art
from the condition of the appetite of the maker: it is not
his good but the good of the work that is in view. An
artist is not praised as an artist because of his appetitive
condition but because the work he makes is good. *Non
enim pertinet ad laudem artificis, inquantum artifex est, qua
voluntate opus faciat; sed quale sit opus quod facit.* (IaIIae, q.
57, a. 3.) This leads Thomas to see an affinity between
art and the speculative virtues. The aim of the latter is
truth and a mathematical argument is assessed without
reference to the moral character of the mathematician.
Summarizing this, Thomas introduces. almost as an
aside, an extremely important point. The virtues of the
speculative intellect and art are *capacities* to do
something well, whether arriving at the truth or
producing good artifacts -- but they do not insure the
good *use* of those capacities. This means that, in order
for the artist to use well the art that he has, he must be
in possession of moral virtues which perfect his
appetites.

The tradition within which Maritain moves sees the
capacity of the artist to produce good artifacts as
independent of his moral condition. There is no
intrinsic dependence of art on moral virtue anymore
than there is an intrinsic dependence of geometry on the
moral character of the geometer or for that matter of
moral philosophy on the appetitive condition of the
moral philosopher. There is such an intrinsic
dependence in the case of prudence or practical wisdom;

:unless a person's appetite is steadily oriented to the true good he cannot have the virtue of prudence. That is why Thomas says that prudence gives both a capacity and its use. The suggestion is that theoretical knowledge and art are amoral.

If the judgment of the artist were to be one by way of affective connaturality, therefore, this would entail that the appetite of the artist is in some way in conflict with the good of the artifact and that he is in need of moral virtue to bring his appetite under control and thereby make the many particular judgments he must make in order to effect the artifact. But Thomas Aquinas, on whom Maritain is relying, does not see this to be the case. The judgment of the artist as he proceeds in his work is not intrinsically dependent on virtues which steadily orient his appetite to the good of the artifact. From this it follows that the judgment of the artist cannot be described as proceeding by way of affective connaturality. No more could one describe the judgments of the geometer or of the moral philosopher as instances of judgments by way of affective connaturality.

From a narrowly exegetical point of view, then, one would have to say that the thought of Thomas Aquinas provides Maritain no basis for speaking of poetic knowledge as an instance of affective connaturality; on the contrary, it prevents him from doing so. Any student of Maritain will know that on many occasions he was confronted with criticism of this sort, someone pointing out to him that the texts of Thomas on which he sought to rely do not sustain the use to which he wished to put them. This was true in political philosophy, philosophy of science, his discussions of degrees of practical knowing, and so on. As often as not, the critics were right. Maritain was working *from* texts of

Thomas, not providing glosses on them, although it must be said that sometimes he himself seemed only imperfectly aware of this.

I want to show that what he had to say of art and morality, which has a good Thomistic textual base, provided him with the opening through which he went on to speak of creative intuition as involving affective connaturality, thereby extending the Thomistic notion of affective connaturality, but not in a way which conflicts with his master, however much he has gone beyond him.

III

The distinction Thomas makes between capacity (*facultas*) and use and his claim that speculative virtues and art give only a capacity and not an inclination to use it well, are in many ways puzzling. On the one hand, he underwrites the obvious fact that a good geometer need not be a good man; on the other hand, he seems to invite the almost excessive divorce of art from human life of the kind we saw in the passage from *Art and Scholasticism* we quoted earlier. There is something unsavory in the suggestion that one has a choice between being a good artist or a good geometer, on the one hand, and a good man, on the other. Furthermore, to do geometry or to write a poem would seem to be instances of human actions and these, we saw, are by definition moral. How can some human activities escape the net of morality if human actions are as such moral? One is reminded of Yeats's poem *The Choice*.

The intellect of man is forced to choose

Perfection of the life or of the work

And if the latter must refuse

A heavenly mansion, raging in the dark.

Maritain himself quotes this poem.

If we begin with the speculative sciences, a way to resolve the difficulty suggests itself. In Chapter 4, I have discussed this in relation to Maritain's notion of Christian philosophy. Doing geometry is a human act and as such is subject to moral appraisal. Let us imagine a mathematician, in his office, at the blackboard, chalking his way toward a proof hitherto unknown to men. He achieves it. On that basis we will say that he is a good geometer. Why does that not suffice for us to call him a good man? Well, let's say that, while he works, his assistant who had been leaning out the window fell and dangles precariously by his fingertips, shouting for help and the geometer ignores him. No achievement in geometry is going to override the misfortune of the assistant who loses his grip and plummets to his death just as the geometer turns from his board and cries, "Eureka!"

The skill or capacity of the geometer is put to use in a context which provides ways of appraising what he is doing in a moral and not a mathematical way. It is the same activity that gets him good grades as a geometer and bad grades as a man. A more morally sensitive geometer does not, on that score, get good grades as a geometer but as a human being. The moral considerations always take priority; they are overriding. At the funeral of his assistant, the geometer cannot justify what he did, or failed to do, by sketching for the widow the proof he was writing on the blackboard the afternoon her husband fluttered down seven stories to become a lifeless messy asterisk on the pavement below. Thus the *use* of his capacity is in the moral order and for the assessment of that the usual moral considerations obtain, including the doctrine of prudential judgments by way of affective connaturality.

This is the sort of consideration we find Maritain undertaking in the final chapter of *Art and Scholasticism* where he discusses art and morality.

> Because it exists in man and because its good is not the good of man, art is subject in its exercise to an extrinsic control, imposed in the name of a higher end which is the beatitude of the living being in whom it resides. (*Op. cit.,* p. 71)

The little book called *The Responsibilities of the Artist* is a later and more thorough discussion of the matter. What has been said of the geometer may be said of the shoemaker or sonneteer. Painting an undraped model in a public park at noonday would require a justification from the artist other than the result on canvas, or at least it would have in a saner day. Taking samples of human skin with a sharp knife in the subway cannot be justified by the artist's claim that he is in search of more realistic pigments. The contralto ought to pay her bills and her high notes do not suffice. The artist is a human being and the common moral demands on human beings apply to him. These demands may dictate that he not practice his art in certain circumstances.

All that is true enough, but it is scarcely interesting. Or at least it would not be if some artists have not wished to fashion a morality controlled by the good of the work alone, everything else being resolutely subordinated to it. Maritain's discussion of Art for Art's Sake, in the little book just mentioned, relies heavily on his personal knowledge of such artists as Jean Cocteau and his readings in others such as Oscar Wilde. He knew that artists have often devised a pseudo-morality, requiring great self-abnegation, even asceticism, with ruthless treatment of others, in order to accomplish the ends of their art. They are a facet of the phenomenon Kierkegaard calls the Aesthete. The Kierkegaardian aesthete is not necessarily an artist in the usual sense. He may simply be a hedonist. But hedonism too makes demands lest one become jaded. There must be a rotation of crops to stave off boredom and retain some novelty in the constantly repeated activity.

This shadow morality, while it does not question the distinctions Maritain has taken from Aquinas, modifies them subtly. The artist can take the end of his art as his supreme good in the way Yeats's poem suggests. Morally evil action may then be justified as providing experience important for the production of artifacts. Wilde, noting that the poet must be able to depict both good and evil, took this to justify the claim that the poet must *be* good and evil.

None of this takes us to the center of Maritain's contention that poetic knowledge involves affective connaturality. But it is the way to the center. The morally good use of the capacity which the virtue of art provides is extrinsic to art as such; it merely places it in the wider human moral context in which art is exercised and enables us to make a twofold assessment of it, intrinsic as art, extrinsic as moral. Maritain wants to argue for more than an extrinsic or *per accidens* connection of morality and poetic knowledge.

> A moral poison which warps in the long run the power of vision will finally, through an indirect repercussion, warp artistic creativity -- though perhaps this poison will have stimulated or sensitized it for a time. At long last the work always *avows*. When it is a question of great poets, this kind of avowal does not prevent the work from being great and treasurable, yet it points to some soft spot in this greatness. [*The Responsibility of the Artists*, Gordian Press, New York, 1972

In Maritain's *The Range of Reason* , one finds essays on artistic judgment and knowledge through connaturality. See as well Rafael-Tomas Caldera, *Le Jugement par Inclination chez Saint Thomas d'Aquin,* Paris, 1980.

There is a refreshing lack of moralizing in Maritain's discussions of the relationship between art and morality. He is not interested in denying that men who are reprehensible human beings nonetheless produce works of art of undeniable excellence. Yet he is attracted by the view that the morally good person, all other things being equal, will be a better artist.

This can mean at least two things, as we have already seen. It can mean that artistic activity is engaged in by a human being and thus comes under a moral assessment as well as an aesthetic one. The discipline required of the artist is itself a moral achievement and can indeed form part of a network of practices which make up his way of life. Maritain will regard this as a shadow morality if the good of the artifact is taken to be the supreme good of the artist as man as well as artist. The undeniable discipline and restraint and asceticism in such a life may be such that the ordinary demands of morality are ruthlessly set aside as conflicting with the good of the work.

But there is a sunnier possibility, Maritain feels, and that is when the moral virtues, while retaining their orientation to the human end *also* facilitate the achievement of the ends of art. And then, speaking of the artist's affinity with his subject matter, Maritain suggests that a parallel can be drawn between art and contemplation. The contemplative enters into affective union with God and this affectivity supplies a cognitive object, a type of knowledge. *Amor transit in conditionem objecti,* as John of St. Thomas put it: the appetitive relation between lover and beloved itself becomes thematic. Here we have the basis of Maritain's prolongation of the notion of affective connaturality to poetic knowledge.

We have also reached the point where Maritain's use of the notion of affective connaturality in speaking of poetic knowledge touches on his use of intuition for the same purpose. Increasingly, his interest turned to the preconceptual or non-conceptual knowledge out of which the fashioning knowledge of the artist arises, the sense of the world and of reality which precedes the constructive work. *Creative Intuition in Art and Poetry*, perhaps the most important single work on aesthetics Maritain wrote, is precisely devoted to this.

IV

The text in Aquinas from which Maritain began, with its distinction between the judgment of the moral philosopher and the judgment of the moral agent, suggests a contrast in aesthetics that Maritain did not draw, namely that between criticism or theory, on the one hand, and practice or production, on the other. The working artist does not require a theory of art anymore than every human agent must have an articulated moral theory. The dependence of criticism on art also emerges from pursuing this parallel. Just as the moral philosopher must presuppose the existence of good men and be guided by them as he develops his theory, so too criticism and aesthetic theory are parasitic on the existence of artifacts. Given the artifact and the ostensible good intended, the critic can assess how well and to what degree the artist has achieved the end he set himself. Finally, just as moral theory has what use it has when it is returned to the order of singular actions from which it takes its rise, so criticism and aesthetic theory are ultimately justified by the way they enhance our appreciation and understanding of art.

Maritain went in a different direction from the passage in question, a direction that finally led him to the view he summarized thus.

> Let me add that the highest form of knowledge through inclination or congeniality is provided by that kind of presences of the one within the other which is proper to love. If the novelist is the God of his characters, why could be not love them with a redeeming love? We are told (it is irrational, but it is a fact), that Bernanos could not help *praying for his characters*. When a novelist has this kind of love even for his most hateful characters, then he knows them, through inclination, in the truest possible way, and the risk of being contaminated by them still exists for him, I think, but to a lesser degree than ever. [*Responsibility*, p. 114.]

A novelist's way of seeing his characters, their hopes and dreams and actions, in short, his vision of life -- is it to this that Maritain would draw our attention? There are many things which contribute to the way an artist, or anyone, sees the world/ The novelist, whatever his vision, must struggle to be true to it, to enable his reader to *see* in Conrad's sense or, in the Hemingway sense of it, to write *truly*. As for the artist's vision, apart from its metabolic, psychological, genetic and other accidental components, there seems room in it as well for an influence from his moral character. Maritain has suggested a number of ways in which the artist's moral character can influence his art. His position remained tantalizing vague. That may be one of its attractions. Who today will dare to carry on the line of investigation Maritain opened up?

TWELVE

MERTON AND MARITAIN

The theme Spirituality in a Secularized Society invites
certain historical reflections which turn out to be far
from tangential to the lives and writings of Jacques
Maritain and Thomas Merton. If I may be permitted an
autobiographical remark, I am especially pleased to
discuss the spirituality of these two men because it was
in the same year, 1948, that I first read *The Seven Story
Mountain* and *An Introduction to Philosophy*. To fall under
the influence of Maritain and Merton was a common
feature of the lives of those of us who were coming of
age in the late Forties and who saw in the great French
Thomist and the fascinatingly congenial Trappist of
Gethsemane vital models as well as mentors. Strange
myths about the decades that preceded Vatican II have
achieved currency. For one who considers that bliss was

it in those days to be alive and very heaven to be young, it is puzzling to hear not only false but condescending remarks about a time that was influenced by Maritain and Merton but also by Chesterton, Belloc, Bloy, Mauriac, Green, Waugh, Claudel, Gilson -- to speak only of kings across the water.

It should be said that there was then a sense of the Catholic intellectual life that was exciting and far from apologetic, an almost romantic attachment to the cultural tradition of the faith, the conviction that "after the surprising conversions," as Robert Lowell put it, cradle Catholics as well as converts would make contributions to the spiritual and cultural life of the nation that would be all the better for being Catholic. Those were the days of Catholic Action, the Renascence Society and the golden days of the Thomistic Revival.

But if Maritain and Merton were part of a vast network of Catholic thinkers and artists who evinced pride in our spiritual and cultural tradition, they were in their different and related ways especially distinctive. Perhaps more than others they spoke of philosophy and poetry as activities to be carried on in the wider context of the life of faith. Both men stressed as definitive the life of prayer; both men laid unusual emphasis on contemplation as the common vocation of the believer.

In the case of Maritain, this emphasis on contemplation may seem somewhat surprising. As A Thomist, Maritain's principal reading was in the works of the great 13th Century Dominican, St. Thomas Aquinas, who seems the telos toward which the previous efforts of Scholasticism aimed. It is the word "scholasticism" that suggests the difficulty. It connotes the work of the schools that developed, as it seemed, away from the interests of the monasteries by finding in secular learning a useful ancillary to their reflections on the faith.

Consider, for example, the kind of opposition that emerges in the 12th Century between such personalities as Peter Abelard and Bernard of Clairvaux. Both men of course were Christian believers, both reflected on what they believed, but Abelard, enthralled by dialectic and in the grips of a species of intellectual triumphalism, seems to see the great documents of belief, Scripture and the Fathers, as occasions for a dazzling intellectual game. In his preface to *Sic et Non*, Abelard lays down a number of useful and interesting principles of interpretation. The work itself is a collection of opposed authorities on a number of crucial issues of Christian belief. Opposition or contradiction is sometimes only apparent -- that is one of the assumptions of the collection -- but even where Scriptural positions are only apparently in conflict, a method is necessary to see that this is so. Martin Grabmann, the great medievalist, sees Abelard as one of the founders of the scholastic method in theology.

The opponents of this method often found it irreverent when they did not see something far worse at work in the writings of people like Abelard. To engage in such dialectical pyrotechnics when confronted by divine revelation seemed as inappropriate as parsing loving letters or checking them for grammatical accuracy. God did not become man in order that men might become theologians. What was needed was a living response to a salvific message, to live a life in the great rhythm of the liturgy, a life of contemplative prayer.

Dialecticians and anti-dialecticians have often opposed one another in the history of Christianity. *The Imitation of Christ* may seem obscurantist and anti-intellectual, but who can be unmoved by the reminder that it is better to feel compunction than to be able to define it? In the 12th Century we see an opposition of monk and schoolman on the matter of scholastic theology. It was Denis the Carthusian who was to ask why so few of those scholastic theologians were raised to the altar while the flow of canonized saints from the monasteries seems uninterrupted.

In recent years, Dom Jean Leclerq has pressed for a rethinking of this opposition, not because he does not recognize the difference between schoolmen and monks, but because he objects to the view that there was no monastic theology. In *The Love of Learning and the Desire for God*, and in many subsequent writings, Leclerq has argued that there is a different and complementary theology coming out of the monasteries. He quotes this passage from St. Bernard on the method of monastic theology

> As for us, in the commentary on mystical and sacred words, let us proceed with caution and simplicity. Let us model ourselves on Scripture which expresses the wisdom hidden in mystery in our own words: when Scripture portrays God for us it suggests Him in terms of our own feelings. The invisible and hidden realities of God which are of such great price are rendered accessible to human minds, vessels, as it were, of little worth, by means of comparisons taken from the realities we know through our senses. Let us also adopt the usage of this chaste language.

This is from the *Sermons on the Canticle of Canticles*. By contrast, all one need do is recall how the scholastic theologian will go on in the 13th century to employ the structure of Aristotelian demonstrative syllogism to speak of theology as a science, argue for the fittingness of using argument in theology and ask whether theology is speculative or practical. Thomas Merton, in *The Last of the Fathers*, put it this way.

Taking a broad, general view of all of Saint Bernard's
writings, we find that they give us a definite and
coherent doctrine, a theology, embracing not merely one
department of Christian life but the whole of that life. In
other words, Saint Bernard is not merely to be classified
as 'a spiritual writer,' as if his doctrine could be limited
to a certain nondogmatic region of affective intimacy
with God. He is spiritual indeed, and a great mystic.
But he is a speculative mystic; his mysticism is expressed
as a theology.

Maritain, in *Les degres du savoir*, traces the modes of
wisdom from natural philosophy through metaphysics
and theology to the mysticism of St. John of the Cross.
That continuum suggests the kind of complementarity
Leclerq speaks of. For Maritain, to philosophize was to
be a Thomist and that meant not only to think as
Thomas did but to live a life like his. Thomas Aquinas
was a mystic, a saint who spent hours in prayer before
teaching and writing, whose whole life was a prayer.
Toward the end of his life, after he had returned to
Naples where his higher studies had begun, Thomas
had the famous mystical experience of which Josef
Pieper wrote in *The Silence of St. Thomas*. The saint
remarked that after what he had seen everything he had
written seemed mere straw and he wrote no more. At
the end of his life he set off for the Council of Lyons, but
fell ill along the way and was taken to the Cistercian
monastery of Fossanova, where he was to die. The
monks asked him to comment on the Canticle of
Canticles. Thomas agreed so long as they would bring
him St. Bernard's sermons on the same book.

We have here an historical backdrop against which to
discuss what Maritain and Merton have to say about
contemplation. *Seeds of Contemplation*, read in the wake

of the tremendous impact of Merton's autobiography, gave us a contemporary and colloquial discussion of matters which might have appeared merely monastic. Yet the author was the same Trappist who was publishing poetry and who was as well -- this should not be forgotten -- a scholar. As John of the Cross had been, Merton was a professor in his monastery.

So too Maritain, first read in the dryly precise *Introduction to Philosophy*, with its definitions and divisions, its sketch of the skeleton of the intellectual enterprise, was the same man one met in the memoirs of his wife Raissa, *We Have Been Friends Together* and *Adventures in Grace*. Moreover, he coauthored with her *Prayer and Intelligence*. The constitution of the *Cercle d'etudes thomistes* which the Maritains conducted at Meudon prior to World War I, stresses the role of prayer and retreats in order to assimilate Thomism and make it a felt force in the cultural life of the France of the time.

Starting, as it may seem, from different points, Maritain and Merton both exhibit rather than merely argue for the complementarity of the two theologies Leclerq describes. More importantly, they relate these theologies to the depths of the Christian life and its full expression in contemplation.

To read Merton's *The Ascent to Truth* is to find oneself in the presence of a scholar of a different valence from Maritain but nonetheless a scholar. Let me now attempt to say a few things about contemplation and the intellectual life, contemplation and the academic life, guided by Maritain and Merton. Indeed, what I have to say is little more than an elaborate gloss on what Maritain means by Christian Philosophy.

In a chapter entitled "Faith and Reason" in *The Ascent to Truth*, we do not find an abstract discussion of two ways of entertaining a truth, on evidence or on authority. Merton proceeds in an anecdotal manner, drawing our attention to some overlooked aspects of the life of St. John of the Cross. The Carmelite mystic was a professor and even served for a time as rector of a theological college of his Order. I am not suggesting that this was an historical discovery Merton made; the fact was well enough known. What is important is the significance he finds in the fact. But what a fact it is. The life of John of the Cross can frighten us. His asceticism strikes *l'homme moyen sensuel* as repellent and even the well disposed may be forgiven for thinking that he is so unlike the rest of men that he can scarcely serve as our model. Perhaps if one had a Carmelite vocation...

The first antidote to this is found in the poetry which, before it is seen as allegorical, has a direct lyrical impact. Merton makes use of the professorial career in much the same way, to humanize his portrait of John. "Under the masterly direction of this saint, Carmelite students at Alcala were living the lives of intellectuals and mystics at the same time -- and finding no contradiction between the two. It is said that in Saint John's time practically all the students at the college were 'great contemplatives.'" (144-5)

Saint Teresa, Merton remarks, had suffered too much from half educated directors; she wanted the priests of the Carmelite reform to be well grounded in theology. Saint John did not see his academic career as in opposition to his vocation as a mystic. Merton quotes the following words of the saint, which he rightly regards as of great significance.

> He (God) draws near to those who come together to treat concerning truth in order to expound and confirm it in them upon a foundation of natural reason.

Merton takes the upshot of this to be that those who consider St. John of the Cross to be the enemy of scholastic thought have fundamentally misunderstood him. "The study of scholastic theology not only is no obstacle to the contemplative life, it is its necessary foundation." (150)

If one sought a parallel to this in Maritain, it would go somewhat differently. One might find Merton's words just quoted a cause for preening, as if unlike other misguided souls one had wisely devoted himself to the study of the great scholastics. But surely there is a possible dark side to the picture. Does it not contain an implicit warning about a concern with scholastic theology which is closed to the possibility of contemplation? Is there not just as much danger in a pursuit of the intellectual life divorced from the spiritual life? To read a monk's warning that out spiritual life may suffer it if its not tied to the intellectual life may not be the advice most of us need. For every person concerned with his soul who eschews the *Summa theologiae*, there may be dozens of academics in whose lives there is either a dissociation of the life of the mind and their faith or an understanding of the intellectual life which almost insures that its pursuit will draw them away from the faith let alone toward the spiritual life.

It was Kierkegaard who said that we have forgotten what it is to be a Christian because we have forgotten what it is to be a man. In the university it is not at all unusual to see young people who, enthralled by the intellectual and existential promise of undergraduate courses, go on to graduate work and find there disillusionment. The trivialization of a pursuit that is one of the natural glories of civilization in the name of professionalism is deeply depressing to the young in the first fervor of their higher studies. The great questions seem fragmented into smaller and smaller ones until they are lost sight of entirely and disputes go on and on over matters of little or no moment. What can I know? What must I do? What may I hope for? So Kant formulated the big questions of philosophy. How often they are treated with methodological skepticism, too vague to deserve an answer. Nowadays a philosopher is embarrassed by the suggestion that he might presume to tell us how to live. Young graduate students do not see any relation between the topics and style of their seminars and the paradigmatic efforts of Plato, Aristotle, Plotinus, Augustine, Boethius, Bede, Anselm, Hugh of St. Victor, Aquinas, Pascal. What do all those men have in common? That they saw a virtuous life as a condition for achieving the truth, that they were trying to be holy as well as wise.

Students will be told that we have made a linguistic turn, that contemporary man knows something that was hidden to those great predecessors, that now at last the philosophical enterprise is carried on as it should be. Well, there is much that is important and interesting in contemporary philosophy, but undeniably for the most part the most important thing of all is missing. Too easily we lose the sense that what is being discussed *matters*, that what is learned is in continuity with the certainties and convictions one brings to philosophy. Debunking seems unserious because it has so little to do with the lives led by the debunkers. Thought is dissociated from the thinker.

Philosophy is a way of life. It is the pursuit of wisdom. It is far more an effort to become a kind of person than it is to learn and know something. The mark of contemporary philosophy is criticism. English bards and Scotch reviewers? Something like that. In *De omnibus dubitandum est*, an unfinished work, Kierkegaard sketched the living absurdity of the view that philosophy begins with doubt, with negativity, with rejection. His suggestion was that philosophy will be redeemed when it regains its link with life and that this redemption will entail a broadening as well as a multiplying of the modes of discourse in which philosophy is expressed.

If the dissociation of thought and life is bad from a natural point of view, how much worse when the life of the mind is divorced from the life of faith. There are professional philosophers for whom there simply is no relation whatsoever between what they professionally do and what they profess to believe. Here is one of the great manifestations as well as sources of current fideism.

> Especially in our times so full of errors and above all where the discipline and graces proper to the religious state are lacking, we think it is impossible that Thomism can be retained in its integrity and purity without the special aid of a life of prayer.

That is taken from the Statutes of the *Cercle d'etudes thomistes* that Maritain printed as an appendix to his *Carnet de Notes*. They are the source of the thoughts expressed here.

There are many alive today who remember when Catholic colleges and universities were strongholds of Thomism, philosophy and theology departments animated by the thought of Aquinas. Something happened. It is no longer thus. What went wrong? Is it possible that we were insufficiently Thomistic rather than too exclusively so? Was an institutional Thomism divorced from the real springs of Thomas's thought? Were those departments of philosophy and theology guided by the outlook expressed in the thought of Maritain just cited?

Let these questions remain rhetorical ones. What is clearly at the center of our tradition, a truth of which both Jacques Maritain and Thomas Merton were witnesses, is this: Unless the intellectual life is seen as a vocation, as a special way of leading the Christian life, it will become a lily that festers and smells worse than weeds. Thomists who pray together stay together? Perhaps. In the Epistle to the Romans, St. Paul attributes the moral turpitude of the pagans to their failure to act appropriately in the light of their natural knowledge of God.

That is the dark side of the picture. The bright and attractive side is this. The great heroes of the Catholic intellectual life have always been holy men and women, saints, mystics. One is a Thomist only in a marginal sense if Thomas appeals only to his mind and not to his soul as well. Much the same can be said of the impact of Jacques Maritain and Thomas Merton. Could anything better be said of them?

APPENDIX

THE THOMISTIC STUDIES CIRCLE

Jacques Maritain published his *Carnet de Notes* in 1965, toward the end of his long life, although eight years and several books would intervene before he died. Still to come were *On the Grace and Humanity of Jesus* (1967) and *Of Christ's Church* (1968), neither of which had the enormous effect of *The Peasant of the Garonne*, published in 1966. The 1966 book made Maritain a controversial figure one more time. Often in the past he had surprised those who thought they knew exactly where he stood. *The Peasant* was a final surprise, reminding those who needed the reminder that Jacques Maritain was a thinker not easily categorizable in terms of superficial or journalistic labels. Looked back to from the stir caused by *The Peasant*, his *Notebook* by contrast has a serene, nostalgic, even valetudinarian, air about it.

The editing of Raissa's journal, which appeared in 1962, had been a labor of love for Jacques. Indeed, he was more than willing to let the journals of his wife suffice for them both; after all, he had called her *dimidium animae meae* -- half my soul. Among her effects were four little notebooks covering the time from 1906 to 1926, a journal for the year 1931, and some loose sheets covering the years 1931 to 1939. Jacques prepared these for the press, added some brief texts from her published writings as well as a letter about Raissa written by their goddaughter Antoinette Grunelius, and seemed content to let that book fulfill his duty to their shared past. To the degree, that is, that the lives of the Maritains could become a public matter.

When Maritain published his own *Carnet de Notes* in 1965, it became clear that Raissa's final illness and death, and the great sense of loss that followed, had interrupted a work begun in 1954. In fact, that ultimate work is made up of geological layers that give it a peculiar fascination.

The basic text consists of chapters composed at a decade's distance from one another and the appendices include materials which date from the times written about in those chapters. Whenever possible, Maritain tells us, he refreshed his memory by consulting small pocket diaries he had kept. Sometimes he actually includes passages from them.

He relies on such pocket diaries when he can because, as he remarks, he destroyed many of the earliest ones. From 1906 to 1911, he kept careful notes and they sometimes became voluminous. "Thereafter I kept little pocket notebooks in an increasingly quick and summary way, several of which were lost." Fewer than he thought, actually. Several of those pocket diaries can be found in the Jacques Maritain Center at the University of Notre Dame.

I have before me as I write Maritain's *Agenda pour 1924*, three inches by five, stiff brown cover, the unnumbered pages printed on graphed paper, each printed date accompanied by the name of the saint of the day. The little diary was bought at *Magasin Reunis*. It is the rare date that does not have an entry of some kind, most of them unreadable, as if Maritain sought to mimick the *litera inintelligibilis* of his master. *Nulla dies sine linea?* Well, some sort of note, anyway, a name, an address, frequently a drawing, always a head, usually as seen from above. More often than not, Maritain made these entries in pencil but they have not faded. His hand is difficult to decipher even when, as in the back of the book, he is writing connected prose. It is easy to imagine that these notebooks would evoke people, events, ideas and images, the past, for the one who kept them. Who could be unmoved at paging through even so modest a relic as this, turning the pages written on by the great Catholic philosopher himself, asking what a reference to a Carmelite convent might mean, wondering why Tea Room occurs like that, in English, and so on.

A somewhat similarly fascinating item in the Maritain Center is Jacques's copy of the *Quaestio disputata de veritate* of St. Thomas Aquinas. The margins are thick with notes and there are loose slips of paper scattered through the two volumes of the work which contain more notes and, of course, outlines. Maritain loved outlines and schemata. Since he was not the kind of Thomist who wrote exegetical studies of the master's works, it is important to see how carefully Maritain read

St. Thomas, assimilating the thought of the Angelic Doctor which would emerge in Maritain's own idiom in his books.

Maritain's *Notebook* contains eight chapters which follow a Foreword written in 1964 and a Preface which dates from 1954. The chapter titles are indicative.

I. Old Memories Prior to Baptism.

II. Old Memories After Baptism.

III . Our First Trip to Rome.

IV. Meeting Pierre Villard.

V. Thomistic Study Circles and Annual Retreats

VI. Our Sister Vera

VII. Love and Friendship

VIII. Apropos of the Heavenly Church

In the 1964 Foreword, Maritain tells us that the first two chapters were written in 1954, the fourth was begun in 1954 and finished in 1961, the fifth was written in 1963 (although the final pages date from 1954), the sixth in 1964, the seventh in 1962, and the last in 1963. The earlier invocation of geological layers to speak of this book was prompted by the dating of its parts.

The Thomistic Study Circles, the subject of the fifth chapter and of a lengthy appendix, flourished from 1919 to 1939 and were one of the casualities of the Second World War. Writing in 1963, Maritain recalls the origins and formal constitution of these circles, dating the first meeting, which took place in their home in Versailles, in the Autumn of 1919, though the seed for the gatherings seems to have been planted in 1914. Some of his students from the *Institut Catholique* as well as some friends came together casually and without plan at first but within a few years the meetings had become a fixture and the idea occurred of establishing them on a formal basis. It was at Meudon that they acquired their special character, bringing together men and women, students and professors, doctors, poets, musicians, businessmen, the majority lay people, but members of the clergy too, the wise and the simple, mostly Catholics but some unbelievers and some Jews, Orthodox and Protestants. Needless to say, some of these categories overlap. What bound them all together? "A deep love of, or an interest large or small in, Thomistic thought."

The atmosphere was not that of a classroom but rather of a salon, with drinks and cigarettes and, at the end, tea.   For a long period of time, the basis of the conversation was a text of St. Thomas or a passage from John of St. Thomas, characterized by Maritain as the last of the great Thomistic commentators. The aim of it all was to bring diverse things into relation with one another -- reason and faith, philosophy and theology, metaphysics, poetry and politics, along with aspects of contemporary culture. Maritain himself would present the topic and the list of those covered is formidable: *Angelic knowledge. How angels know future contingents, singular things and secrets of the heart. Intellectual knowledge. Is what sense is sociology a science? Practical knowledge. Justice and friendship. The Trinity.* And so on. Maritain recalls his wife's remark in *We Have Been Friends Together* that his fidelity to scholastic jargon was undeviating, and he quotes Charles Du Bos to the effect that his vocabulary was unintelligible save to an infinitesimal few. Surely Maritain exaggerates. What comes through to the reader is the level of intellectual excitement these meetings sustained.

When he quotes from notebooks kept at the time, Maritain records the following. "Members must state their intention of being guided by St. Thomas in complete fidelity, to read the *Summa* at least half an hour a day and to pray for at least a half hour daily." No other single sentence could better convey the spirit of these Thomistic Circles. Prayer and understanding, a blending of the spiritual and intellectual lives, the quest of sanctity through the degrees of wisdom. Little surprise that there grew up the custom of annual retreats for the members. Reginald Garrigou-Lagrange, the great Dominican Thomist, with whom Maritain would later have political disagreements, gave the first retreat. Toward the end, two to three hundred people took part in these retreats. Maritain concludes the fifth chapter with a lengthy discussion of the Vow of Prayer.

In recent years such phenomena as the founding of the Fellowship of Catholic Scholars and, more ecumenically, the Society of Christian Philosophers, are partial responses to the needs addressed by the Thomistic Study Circles. Organization has of course its repellent side, nor was Maritain without a joke about that side of the effort. Imagine Pascal, he writes, or for that matter, in a different age, a Chateuabriand or a Joseph de Maistre, imagine a Doistoevsky, a Leon Bloy, a Peguy or a Bernanos, organized in teams of common effort! Impossible to conceive. Whatever good the *Cercles* did, Maritain would not permit himself or others to forget what unorganized and unorganizable Christians can and have done.

That being said, there is a need on the part of those with seemingly a double vocation to come together. It was the effort to unite those bent on living the life of the mind and the life of the soul, the intellectual and spiritual lives, that characterized the *Cercles*. The little book Jacques and Raissa co-authored, *La vie d'oraison -- Prayer and Intelligence* in English --addresses the same ideal. This conviction that development of the mind must go hand in hand with development of spirit is the single most important element of the influence Jacques Maritain continues to have.

Here is a portion of the appendix to the fifth chapter of the *Notebook*.

STATUTES OF THE THOMISTIC STUDY CIRCLES

O SAPIENTIA

O Sapientia, quae ex ore

Altimissimi prodiisti, attingens

a fine usque ad finem

fortiter, suaviterque

disponens omnia: veni ad

docendum nos viam

prudentiae.

I. General Principles

1. In making Saint Thomas Aquinas the Common Doctor of the Church, God has given him to us as our leader and guide in the knowledge of the truth. The doctrine of Saint Thomas is the one the Church recommends above all others and enjoins her masters to teach. It imposes itself on the mind as a chain of certitudes demonstratively linked and more than any other is in perfect accord with dogma. It possesses the proof of a holiness inseparable from the teaching mission of the Angelic Doctor which causes a sort of effacement of his human personality in the radiance of the divine light. As Leo XIII wrote, "Having profoundly venerated" the Fathers and holy doctors who preceded him, Saint Thomas "inherited as it were the intelligence of them all." He so lost himself in the truth that one can

say of him, as one of his greatest students did: *Majus aliquid in sancto Thoma quam sanctum Thomam suscipitur et defenditur: it is something far greater than Saint Thomas that we accept and defend in Saint Thomas.* Inheritor of the past and treasure of the future, he alone can teach us to become, following his example as much as our weakness permits, transparent to the truth, docile to the Spirit who gives understanding, open to the common and catholic wisdom with which the Church has been imbued. An active loyalty, progressive and conquering, but absolutely pure and whole, to the principles, doctrine and spirit of Saint Thomas is thus the means par excellence of serving the Truth who is Christ; and it is particularly needed for the salvation of the understanding, today threatened on all sides.

2. Along with that, we believe that human understanding is by nature so weak and has been furthered weakened by Original Sin, and the thought of Saint Thomas is so intellectually demanding, both philosophically and theologically, that in order for us to assimilate his thought we need all the supernatural grace and help of which both the eminent holiness as well as the unique mission of the Angelic Doctor assure us and that the special help of the Holy Spirit is and always will be necessary for it to live among men.

In our error-filled time, we particularly believe that where the discipline and graces proper to the religious life do not obtain, it is impossible for Thomism to be maintained in its integrity and purity without the special help of a life of prayer.

We know that this union of the spiritual life and the life of study was not only achieved in an eminent degree by Saint Thomas himself, but also by his most authoritative commentators, like Banez, the spiritual director most prized by Saint Teresa, like Gonet, who dedicated his *Clypeus thomisticae theologiae* to the great contemplative, like the Masters of Salamanca (*Salmanticenses*) who remained loyal on all points of Thomistic theology and who saw in it the foundation of

the great spiritual doctrines taught by Saint Teresa and
by Saint John of the Cross.

3. Thomism, thanks to the powerful impulse given by
Leo XIII, has already begun to win minds among
diocesan clergy and lay people, and is destined to do so
more and more. How else can it conquer modern
understanding? It must permeate the dough in order to
raise it. In order to continue in time and renew
philosophy while assimilating what has been acquired
since the Middle Ages and directing its progress into all
domains, disengaging the true meaning of all the partial
truths and research accumulated by particular sciences,
to animate and clarify the intellectual renaissance which
is possible in the realm of arts and letters whose role
could be immense and, finally, to shape the general
understanding which more than ever needs a general
philosophical and theological culture -- to do all that,
Thomism must enter into the intellectual life of those
who life in the world, of lay people, and find
practicioners there.

Its very diffusion can give rise to dangers. To the
degree that modern minds which are insufficiently
armed and prepared and more or less under the influence
of modern prejudices seek to examine it, it runs the risk
of being studied in an inappropriate light and thereby
subjected to diminished, partial and deforming
interpretations. Experience shows that the danger of the
materialization of Thomism is not imaginary.

4. In order to promote the teaching and the spirit of
Saint Thomas in the world, taking account of the
dangers just mentioned and maintaining the Thomistic
synthesis in the higher light it requires, it thus seems
useful and opportune that souls of good will who, out of
love of Truth and the Church, wish to work for the
diffusion of Thomism or just to be inspired by it, be
united in study circles which will help them perfect their
knowledge of Saint Thomas, make it better known, and
help preserve the living tradition of the masters of
Thomism among the laity in an enduring way.

5. The chief element being, as we have seen, the spiritual and supernatural one and such a group being valuable and effective only if its members are open in the fullest way to the action of the Holy Spirit, every member must be bound by a private vow to devote himself to a life of prayer. In that way this group of diocesan priests and lay people will have at the base of their activity a profound and intimate gift of self to God and will offer to souls who aspire to perfection in the world a very real aid without in any way interfering with anyone's freedom since the vow of prayer concerns only the absolutely personal relation between God and the soul.

The usefulness of the study circles is twofold. On the one hand, they will help maintain with integrity and purity the renewal of Thomistic studies in this century by means of prayer and, on the other hand, they will help maintain the renewal of spirituality in this century in rightness and purity by means of Thomism.

In an age when the majority is interested in anything but God and seems to have lost the capacity to rise to the First Cause, it seems desirable that members include in their intentions that of *intellectual reparation*. For if it is true that intellectuals have in a special way the duty to recognize in God the supreme object of understanding and to ponder with love and reverence the depths of natural and supernatural theolgy, it is equally true that God is in our time especially offended by them. Therefore it is necessary that intellectuals devote themselves in a special way to giving God the homage refused him by modern philosophers and at the same time to intercede for those who are the willing or unwilling victims of error.

There follows a second longer part having to do with the organization of the various circles which goes into great detail concerning their activities. To read Maritain's *Motebook* on such matters, his later reflections interspersed with notes made at earlier times, and then to read these statutes is to receive a powerful sense of his vision of what it means for a Catholic to be devoted to the life of the mind. The centrality of the role of Saint Thomas Aquinas could scarcely be more dramatically emphasized. Some may find all this frightfully preconciliar. They may think that the days of the influence of Thomas Aquinas are behind us. They are wrong. But if Thomas is to continue to play a central role in Catholic intellectual and cultural life, this will only be in the way laid down by Jacques Maritain as he recounts the story of the Thomistic Study Circles.

INDEX

200

202